Fourteen Hills

Vol. 13 No. 1
2007

*The San Francisco State
University Review*

Acknowledgements.

Fourteen Hills would like to thank the following for help and support in putting this issue together:

Maxine Chernoff	Paul Sherwin
Jennifer Daly	Barbara Eaton
Donna de la Perriere	The Gold Cane
Robert Glück	Peter Orner
Jason Snyder	Brian Thortenson
Thomas Guynes	Truong Tran
Richard Uchida	Rapid Copy
Rita Hernandez	

Credits.

Cover artwork: *At the moment of launch, the quick release jammed and Huffaker lost his cool* by Ethan Murrow.
Graphite on paper, 72in. x 144in., 2006.
Cover design & text composition: Michael McCurdy & Maria Suarez

Distributed by.

Small Press Distribution, Berkeley, Calif. / www.spdbooks.org
Ubiquity Distributors, Inc., Brooklyn, New York / www.ubiquitymags.com

ISSN: 1085-4576
ISBN: 1-889292-13-3

Fourteen Hills is published by the Creative Writing Department at San Francisco State University, with the support of the Instructionally Related Activities Fund.

Fourteen Hills

Vol. 13 No. 1
2007

Maria Suarez
Editor-in-Chief

Jenny Pritchett
Managing Editor

Matthew Davison
Faculty Advisor

Antonio Fernandez
Asst. Managing Editor

Laura Moore
Poetry Editor

Tom Robinson
Fiction Editor

Rae Freudenberger
Asst. Poetry Editor

Radhika Sharma
Asst. Fiction Editor

Editorial Staff.

Seth Fragomen • Jami Frush • Daniel Johnson
Lusine Khachatryan • Anna Lonnberg
Alex Muramoto • Matthew Rohrer
William Weston • Laura Wolfe • Roberta Wood

Fourteen Hills is published twice yearly in San Francisco, Calif.

Subscriptions:
Individual — One year for $17 or two years for $32.
Single issues $9.

Submissions should be accompanied by a self-addressed, stamped envelope. We have a rolling submissions policy, so you may submit at any time, but the cutoff for inclusion in our issue is September 1; for the Fall issue, February 1. All correspondence should be addressed to the appropriate editor at *Fourteen Hills,* c/o the Creative Writing Department, San Francisco State University, 1600 Holloway Ave., San Francisco, CA 94132. *Fourteen Hills* does not accept unsolicited electronic submissions.

www.14hills.net

Contents.

FEATURED ARTIST / ETHAN MURROW / 81-96

FEATURED FICTION / RAY NOLAN / 97-121

Fourteen Hills

Sunday Rest

Theodore Rigby
from *Migrant Workers in South Korea*

Green Makes Red Sing

Robert Strong

Green makes red sing in this painting. French dream a still life with stolen stop sign. Put roses on top a cold tree. Felonious, one supposes, art. One's brain will be red with it, initially. Gray. Then green. The splinter cells do their own thinking, sticking to the general concept. Nothing can be caught that's not communicating or in transit. Stop signs are more like points of asking—a question against the procession. Nor can the go that green gives be ignored. There's still some life in this. The immobile, anonymous man is mythic & impotent. Mad poet, sad-seeming nibbler of radish. The real war is on reverie, the thinking dream that is seamless green & red together. It makes the man nervous to guard a stretched servant whose stare belies a massive character. The giftstore says: *Masculine endings dominate, terminating each cadence with a hard, dull thud lacking elasticity and echo, coming from an accelerated movement to fall head first at the last syllable is not alleviated here by any artifice.* They arrest you in the Met. The tension of getting away with a painting intact through this crowd in mind is too much, two colors. Put your hands inside your head and step out from the frame, sir.

Symmetries

Linh Dinh

Talking constant shoot, he forced the darn
Nude bleep bleep to smear loads on himself.
Later, when chased, he incontinently fled.

Scoring often, he refined his bitchin' techniques,
Flew freakin' home and stabbed her 76 times.

No fireworks, please, or he'll shoot in his dockers.

2084

Bone soap, pubic hair cigs, grass tea,
We make do with milk substitute, egg
And sperm substitute, shit substitute.

Shit, ma, ain't got shit
To eat round here, not even
Some jive shit. [haiku]

Only the barest few, buck naked, can afford nothing.

I was cleaved from my wife, kids, and refrigerator,
Then cleaved from my own bones. Whew!

Beaming happy eyes around a yew tree,
Last one in the hemisphere, apparently.

What's a slipper bath? What's an 8-track player?
What's a lug wrench? What's a rearview mirror?

Luke John

Deborah Eshenour

My name is Luke John Padgett. I'm called Luke John, both names together. My mama named me that after a song she used to sing in Sunday school that went, "Matthew, Mark, Luke and John, Luke and John, Luke and John." That was her favorite song, little Annelle's favorite song, and she thought it would be prettier if the "and" wasn't between "Luke and John," so when she had me, she called me Luke John without the "and." For the past eleven months, right after I started the first fire, I've been trying to get people to call me Luke or L.J. It's not working, though. I thought it would look better for when I published a book on geology, although I don't care as much since I'm not allowed to study geology anymore. I guess you can't be surprised when you live in a little town like Shipman where you know almost everybody and they are used to calling you Luke John for seventeen years. It certainly isn't catching on with the people I see most, like all the old ladies at the Church of the Flock, the same church that my mama Annelle went to since she was a little kid, the same one that she sang that song about the apostles or disciples or whatever they are—she'd be mad if she knew I didn't know the difference, after all I've gone to church three times a week for my whole life. She'd pull her mouth down on one side so that it dug into her cheeks until it looked like that Cabbage Patch doll that my sister Ruth used to have before she died of leukemia. Mama'd pull down her mouth like she does whenever I have the nerve to wear that Harley Davidson t-shirt that Bobby R. gave me. Today it's Tuesday and Bobby R. is out of town visiting his cousin, but he's coming back on Thursday and then him and me are going up to the rock quarry. My mama thinks that anybody who rides motorcycles is doubtless into drinking alcohol and smoking cigarettes and sometimes if she's feeling fired up enough to say the word "hell," she'll say what my grandaddy used to say, which is that fast cars'll getcha into hell quicker (I guess that includes motorcycles). Which isn't even clever or anything, the only reason that it causes such a stir is that it has the word "hell" in it and everybody in my family, all Independent Baptists (Southern Baptists say "hell" and don't go to church on Wednesday nights like we do in the Church of the Flock), is real against cursing of any kind along with most everything else. And so, somehow, it's like that Harley Davidson shirt means that I am drinking, smoking, and causing my mama to curse. Bobby R. drinks and smokes, but I always just act like I'm not interested when he offers me a beer, because I know what beer does to the inside of your liver, Mr. Jeff taught me that. What I did do, after Ruth's death and everything, was start some fires up in the woods behind our house. They were mostly little ones; I'd just burn up some weeds or a bush. It's kind of like an experiment in a way, you light the match and depending on what you put the flame to, you'll get results of different colors before the black ash, different crackly and hissing noises. That last one got out of control, though, cause the wind was blowing and gave the fire a lot of oxygen, and it was beautiful and I was kind of trying to put it out, but just mostly looking at it, letting the hot air blow onto my skin, making me feel alive. But nobody knows about that, cause, and I don't know if this was God hoping I'd never do anything like that again or Satan trying to make it so I was free to get in more trouble, it started raining like you wouldn't believe, just pouring down nails of water, and since

Mama never goes up into our woods, she's not going to notice a few burnt down trees.

Anyway, all the ladies at the Church of the Flock always look real surprised when I tell them I want to be called Luke or L.J., even though I've been telling them now for a long time. They just get that look that old people get, that makes you think they might be a little bit stupid, but you know it's just cause they are getting old and that's how old people get, old and senile and can't remember when anybody wants to be called by just one name or at least initials. And then I get mad at them, and I hate Mrs. Fridley with her watery eyes and Mrs. Shifflett with her white hair with the blue in it from trying to dye her hair at home and her shaky spotty hands and hate how they say they are so proud of me that I'm going to be a preacher one day. And then I feel bad, a pull in my stomach, deep down from somewhere like my own personal hell inside of me, like I might cry, thinking about how these old ladies were so nice to me and my mama when Ruth died a year ago. They brought cakes and pies and stewed cabbage and broccoli casserole and barbequed chicken and so much good food to our old one story rickety house, but I didn't feel like eating.

When Ruth died, Mr. Jeff came over to the house, which is the first time Mama even noticed him since she'd been so wrapped up in Ruth being sick. Mr. Jeff teaches science at Shipman High School and lots of times on Saturdays, him and me would go looking for fossils. Science is the only thing I'm good at, and Mama used to like that, saying that I was honoring God by understanding photosynthesis and what the man-made name of rain clouds is (nimbus). I love science, because it explains what's going on. When something happens to somebody, an autopsy will show what happened to them, and you can't just up and blame death on God or somebody else or whatever. Science makes things rational and keeps things under control. Mr. Jeff said I was his most promising student, even if I do have some learning disabilities, and had me applying for all kinds of colleges that have good science programs. I got accepted to Virginia Tech, but Mama wouldn't hear of it. She did not like Mr. Jeff, because he had us kids call him Mr. Jeff instead of Mr. Hallett, which was his last name. Calling grownups by their first name is not following the Bible's rule to honor your elders. But mostly, she didn't like him because of the geology he taught, because geological calculations of the earth's age are in direct contradiction with the Bible's calculations, which says the world is only a few thousand years old. Also, fossils support the theory of Charles Darwin's evolution, which is heresy. So while I studied with Mr. Jeff for three years through Biology and Physics and Geology, after Ruth died and Mama started asking about all the fossils in my room and the acceptance letters from places like Virginia Tech, she got started on putting an end to all that.

Mama doesn't like anything that isn't something she herself does every day of her life or if it's not something she's heard condoned in the pulpit or knows our pastor does. Like, when Ruth was still living and one of her friends wanted her to go bowling with her and her family, Mama said no and kept saying no until Ruth, who was already sick then, cried to Pastor James and he came over and talked Mama into it, and he had to even say that he'd stop in to make sure they weren't listening to hard rock music or that people weren't drinking beer or anything. Pastor James said maybe Mama's too hard on us sometimes, well, just me now, but told me she just wants to keep me out of trouble, since Mama stayed after church one day to tell him I'd been hanging out with Bobby R., whose family the Ransons are bad news around this town.

Mama's calling me to supper. She sounds mad so she might have been yelling for awhile.

———

So, it's later tonight and Mama's already in bed, even though it's not even nine, probably wearing the same old housedress she wore all day, up in that big brass bed that belonged to my grandparents before they died. There's not much to do at our house because we don't have a television and since Mama took my science books away, I have been just staring out the window or going for walks in the woods. Since I graduated I especially notice how there's nothing to do because I guess before I was always doing science homework or looking for fossils or maybe taking care of Ruth. Now I'm just waiting on seminary school to start in August. The place I'm going is in Tennessee, and I get kind of sick whenever I think about going. I didn't even want to go, if I couldn't go study at Virginia Tech, I wanted to stay here with Pastor James, but he's taught me every summer since I started high school, and he says that he thinks my spiritual needs require someone better than him. Mama took that to mean that I was spiritually mature, but I think it's because Pastor James didn't know what to say to me sometimes. Like, I cry sometimes since Ruth died and men don't like to watch other men cry. Also, I tried to tell Pastor James about how I keep wanting to start fires and how I do light little ones sometimes. He just kind of changed the subject, but maybe he didn't understand what I was getting at. I just feel like I want the feeling in my stomach to go somewhere else, and when I look at fire the feeling is relieved some.

If she knew about it, Mama would say starting fires is an influence of hanging out with Bobby R., but it's not. Bobby R. has set behind me every class my whole life, since Ranson is right behind Padgett alphabetically, and there's no Ps or Qs where we live in Shipman to come between us. I knew since I was born that I wasn't supposed to talk to any Ransons. My Mama has a lot of subjects that she talks on all the time and most of them are about God and sinners or stuff my granddaddy did in his life, but one of them's about the Ransons. They are trash that runs around going to beer joints and some of them are on welfare and they are just a lot of sinners. That's what Mama says anyway, but I don't know how she knows that much, since nobody in the church talks to them. Anyway, Bobby R.—he's called Bobby R. because of Bobby Thornton, who's called Bobby T.—has always set behind me, and I liked that, because like me, he never dressed too well. Both of us got made fun of at different times for the way we dressed, so I always liked him for that, for making me feel not so alone, even though he didn't get called Jesus freak like I did. I don't know why his parents didn't have the money to buy him nice clothes, especially if they were on welfare and all, but my Mama lives off my daddy's pension and so my clothes either belonged to him or my granddaddy or come from the Salvation Army. My daddy was a truck driver, although Mama doesn't like me to say that since most truck drivers take pills and fornicate. He wrecked his truck off a bridge in Wyoming before Ruth was born. The newspaper clippings in our photo album said the side of his rig left a perfect imprint on the concrete support of the bridge. The end of the trailer got stuck on the railing, and the rig just swung like a pendulum into the bridge leg. I always wanted to go see that, the mark my daddy made, but Mama said absolutely not, that if anything I could go clean his grave down at the cemetery behind the church, which is not even a mile from our house.

Bobby R. likes fossils too, and that's how we started being friends. At first he didn't like science at all, but we kept being lab partners and to get a good lab grade so I could get a scholarship to a good science school one day I started helping him understand how everything worked. Bobby R. was smart as anybody, he just never tried, and of course since he comes from a no-good family and wears cut off sleeve t-shirts nobody even thinks he can do anything. But once he started trying, we two had the highest grades and would always do the experiments two or three times while everybody else just did it once. Bobby R. knew that me and Mr. Jeff went looking for fossils and he asked to go along, so we all went to Crabtree Falls one time, and Bobby R. found a trilobite and he was hooked after that. Sometimes when my Mama'd told me to come straight home after school, Bobby R. just begged me to come with him to go look for fossils. If Ruth hadn't been sick at home on the living room sofa I would've. Sometimes when Ruth was in the hospital and Mama stopped caring where I was, Bobby R. and I'd go up to the rock quarry on his motorcycle. That was the most fun I ever had. I liked being with Mr. Jeff and I learned a lot when I was with him, but something about riding on that motorcycle, with my short hair bristles being rubbed by the wind and watching the road underneath go by so fast and the sky kind of stay the same, all that and then going to find fossils, that was the best.

———

It's Wednesday night and I can barely sit still in church. It's prayer meeting tonight, so after the short sermon, everybody gets a chance to pray out loud, and everybody does, except me, and that takes about two hours. Most of the time I'd bring a fossil or two in my pocket and I'd have plenty of time to look it over from every angle. Since Mama got rid of all my fossils, though, I just sit there, time lasting forever. It's lucky that she doesn't open her eyes for nothing so she can't see me staring up at the ceiling or out the window, although she did look at me funny tonight when I sat down in the hard pew behind her and not beside her like I usually do. She let me alone, though, cause earlier when I couldn't even eat dinner and she started getting on me about it, I started to cry into my plate and I couldn't stop until I was crying like a little kid who can't catch his breath. She didn't say anything, just sat and watched, but she looked scared. Now I feel numb, like I can't even move for all the pressure that comes from outside and from my brain and settles down into my stomach.

I've been feeling like this since Ruth died, since Mama said that my studying science was heresy, that my interest in fossils supported evolution and that God had punished us through striking down my little sister because of my unbelief. Pastor James tried to tell her that even though sometimes God does punish people through the death of family members like he did Job, that God probably didn't kill Ruth because I was studying science. He pointed out that the Bible doesn't say exactly how old the earth is, so maybe Mr. Jeff was right when he said it was ten thousand years old and that it's possible to be a scientist and not be an evolutionist. Mama didn't buy it of course and if the subject of science even comes up in the house, she starts sobbing about how my little sister Ruth should still be alive today. Then she usually starts screaming that it's all my fault.

The sermon tonight was about the sanctity of life, how God cherishes human life above everything. Everybody says life is beautiful, but I know that's not true. It's not when you don't have any friends to share it with. But lucky for me I have Bobby R. Life's not beautiful when you are dying of leukemia and you turn into a bald red-eyed gnome like Ruth did, screaming in pain all the time and not understanding most of what you said to her. I think about what she looked like laying in her casket, after looking like she was in the Holocaust for the last year of her life, she looked real pretty in the casket, cause all of her ruined blood had been drained out of her and she had a wig of real hair.

Just like Luke and John was beautiful, before I was alive, before the "and" was gone, before the song was gone. Now it's just a bad name, a dorky name that belongs to some guy who wears old oxford shirts from the Salvation Army and too short corduroys and whose Mama thinks he killed his own sister.

What is beautiful is death. When things aren't living, when they dry up or fossilize or imprint other dead things with their image, then that is beautiful. Then there's no snot or pee or blood, after all the skin and organs have disintegrated. The real beauty is the framework, the bones, the teeth. They are white and smooth and comforting, just like those bones dug from that

Indian grave over in Lovingston. Mr. Jeff brought a skull and an arm bone to class, and I couldn't stop rubbing them, looking at them. They were so quiet and peaceful. That's kind of what I see when I look at fire, if it would just stay still, you can see, in the flickering, little flames of that peace that is death.

I hope when Bobby R. gets back tomorrow that we can ride on his motorcycle and go look at fossils without Mama knowing.

———

It's Thursday afternoon and Bobby R. just called. Lucky for me, Mama was out in the garden picking tomatoes and didn't hear the phone ring. Bobby R. wants to go the quarry tonight, and I am disappointed because you can't look for fossils in the dark. Also I am disappointed because Bobby R. brought his cousin Mickey back with him, and, since he has a motorcycle too, we are going riding. I was hoping it would just be me and Bobby R., but I'm still glad we're going riding.

Bobby R. has told me about his cousin Mickey a lot. He tells how at night they'd drive their motorcycles just about three or four feet apart, right together so they look like car headlights. Then when another car is coming they'll drive up on the car like they are going to hit it, and all the driver of this car sees is the headlights of another vehicle coming right for him. Right when he thinks he's about to die, then Bobby R. and Mickey split up, swerving apart to let the car go in between them. Bobby R. says usually those people stop their cars and yell and scream out the window, but Bobby R. says if that was him that he'd just be glad he was alive, that he made those people appreciate their lives. If it was me, I'd be disappointed. After all, if you hit a car head on, the worst would always be behind you.

I can't wear my Harley shirt tonight, because Mama will see me, so I'll just have to wear my least scratchy oxford short sleeve shirt and hope she doesn't say anything when I tell her I'm going walking in the woods.

———

I have a terrible headache this morning, and I feel like I'm going to throw up, too. I think Bobby R.'s cousin Mickey talked me into drinking some beers last night. I need to stay in bed, but Mama's yelling for me.

Bobby R. came by a while ago. He said he waited until he saw Mama leave to walk to the store before he stopped by. Mama almost didn't go to the store, because she said she's worried about me. The feeling in my stomach has moved up to my neck, which feels like it might snap in two. I know some of it's the beer.

Bobby R. said Mickey kept saying I was a "plumb crazy bastard" last night because he thought I was dressed so weird that I was a sissy boy, and so he was going to scare the living shit out of me, that's what Bobby R. said. So they made me ride on the back with Mickey, and Mickey kept swerving around and acting like he was going to run into things head on. And he was leaning the motorcycle so far down on its side when we went around curves in the road that that's how my pants got torn. But the whole time I didn't ask him to stop or nothing, and Mickey was impressed, but kind of freaked out because he said something was wrong with somebody that wasn't scared even a little bit.

Then Bobby R. said that we all had some beers and that after awhile I started crying and saying that God punished me by taking away my sister and my chance to go to Virginia Tech and that Mama didn't see that our life wasn't beautiful that Mama didn't see and that I hated her, and I wished she was dead so she couldn't say things like I killed my sister. Bobby R. said that I said I wanted to be dead. That I was screaming it.

Bobby R. was squirming in his seat like Pastor James did when I tried to tell him about the fires. If Mama saw his dirty jeans on her old sofa that Ruth died on, she'd hit the roof. But Bobby R. is looking at me closer than Mama ever does. He is saying that one of his cousins was suicidal once and that he went to the UVA psychiatric hospital in Charlottesville, and he got a lot better and was fine now with two kids and a job as a welder. Bobby R. tried to talk more, but I was really worried that Mama would be back, and plus over top of the pressure in my stomach and my neck I was embarrassed that he could see all this stuff about me, so I told him he'd better go. He told me to call him and wrote down his number in case I'd lost it since I'd never called him. It made me want to cry.

It's night now and Mama's asleep. My matches that I had with me last night got wet somehow so it hasn't been easy to get them lit. But after the third try, my bedspread finally caught on fire. It smells really bad—the tag says it's polyester—this is a new experience, because I am used to burning natural things. It's always nice to try different things and compare the results of the experiments. I'm sitting out in the hallway now because the smoke's getting pretty thick, and I am sweating from the heat. I feel relieved, though. Relieved because I have my Harley shirt on and it's comfortable and my skin can breathe. The pressure is lifting, cause I know I don't have to go to seminary school in Tennessee. I don't have to be embarrassed about my clothes anymore, and I don't have to worry about having killed my sister, because I'll be dead, too. In a few hours, most of my body will be ash, and all that will be left is those smooth, smooth bones and teeth, all the mushy decaying flesh and blood burned away. I hear my Mama yelling for me, cause the smell of smoke has caused her to wake up. I am going to go keep her in her bed, I can do it because I can see in the flames the promise of rest. Because if Mama gets help and makes this stop, then she'll make me out to be a suicidal sinner, destroying what God has given both of us. But I'm just making sure that the worst is behind us, leaving only my smooth white bones.

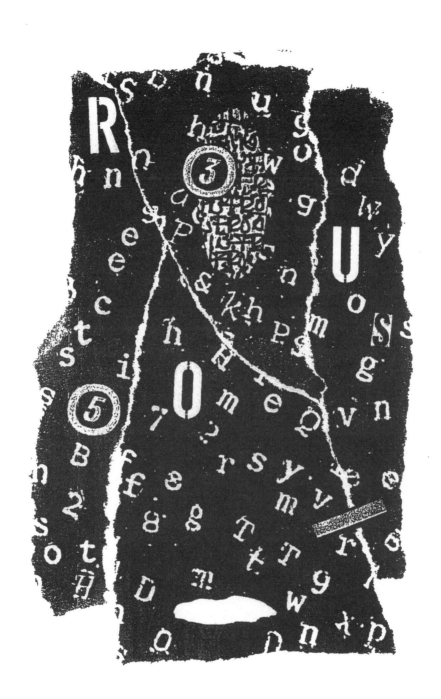

The Dress

Pete Spence

The Rodin Museum

Bronwen Densmore

We come from everywhere to look at them: individuals
who have never been curious want to pull back the statues' lips
and delve for bones; discover the fossil evidence of breath.
We want inside.
We have never been good in bed, but we want to fuck the Rodins,
we can imagine pulling scarves across the throats of dancers
as they pose, powder black and muscular as eels,
we want to wrestle nude women off of suede couches
and abscond in carriages drawn by horses that sweat
and jerk at the bit. This desire is august and unbearable.
When we dream we dream forests of wrists and dark channels
of blood, or of the tendons that make the feet spring.
We have seen angels quarried from wet earth, massive
and shot through with veins. The memory of the Rodins dogs us.
Touch us. . .
And we're trying to, scratching away. There are armatures
submerged in blocks of stone, mallets to tap out shoulders
where the roots of wings might be.

Ambition

Kirsten Andersen

When the Western sun sets on top of the calendar year
it kicks into gear a national opera, where the orphans to Christ
and the American church give praise to their parents and guardians.
The free wheeling face of a dark cloud descends and the workers
sit down to task, winding back the delicate arms of antique
kitchen clocks, stocking warehouse shelves with products
that malfunction. Human as we are in our flesh vessels, keeping pace,
making mark, a man gets tired of moving. He sees a mouth running low
on color, a neighbor spent in the head who is stepping out from town.
A note to the well rested and affluent—we are tired of cats and dialogue,
the tales of easy money, your town cars, the tour bus—which limit
our appreciation of modest pleasure. Here in the modern cage with all
its slippery delights, we ask you for more time. Paycheck to paycheck,
ordinary life, there are rainforests full of feathers in our dreams.

Bad Behavior

Years ago I was granted a pass to participate in bad behavior.
I was instructed by a shortlist of my mother's youngest boyfriends;
they gave me paper and blade, red meat on a bone, taught me
to pepper my beloved with bitter-ended questions. My mother
stood at the freezer drawer and tossed them raspberry popsicles,
while the even handed facts of our survival took shape.
I think of all the men she has packed away in ice, stored in sawdust,
her shoeboxes stuffed with photographs, love letters marked
with prehistoric dates. At the college I sit behind the dean's desk
and catalog quotations. Men who were schooled privately begin
to look at me and I am always fearful, laying the groundwork
to forestall eventually seeming a fool. Entire in my body, I am only
myself, little pockets of a hometown hanging all along my bones.

An Elegy to Roadkill

Keya Mitra

The first burial took place during Leena's third date with Emerson. They were in his car on the way to the movies when Emerson said: "Have you ever thought about cutting your hair short? I had an Indian friend once, and her hair got bushy when it grew beyond a certain length. It looks like you have the same problem."

Leena said nothing and added narcissism to her mental record of Emerson's flaws. *It wouldn't have worked anyway, she thought.* They'd been set up through mutual friends in Houston, and so far Leena had found him unremarkable. Over the years her standards had dwindled, and her level of desperation escalated to an all-time high last week on her thirtieth birthday. After her father's death a year earlier, she'd been delegated the burden of looking after her mother by default; she had no brothers or sisters to share the task. Her mother's desire for grandchildren just barely beat out her passion for dominating her daughter's life, and Leena was frantic to find a husband and escape from the oppressive confines of her home. But even though her mother claimed to only want a "nice, decent boy" for Leena, it was understood that to fit these criteria the man needed to come from a respected Indian family, possess considerable height—preferably over six feet—and have a degree from a law program or medical school, if not both. Not only was Emerson not Indian, he was 5′8 (if that), worked with computers, said "youz" instead of "you," and flaunted a tattoo of his last dog, a Bassett hound, on his right bicep. Leena was about to deliver her usual break-up speech when her body lurched forward, and Emerson slammed on the brakes.

"God—what was that?" Leena asked. Emerson swerved to the side of the road without answering. He grabbed a couple of plastic Kroger bags from the back seat and slammed the car door shut behind him. He walked over to a bloody pile on the street.

It was a black Labrador Retriever with a flattened body and a face indistinguishable from its torso. "Someone hit the poor dog," he called to her. He took off his brown corduroy jacket and crouched in the street, using the two plastic bags as gloves to lift up the animal. He wrapped the arms of the jacket around the corpse before carrying it to the car and depositing the body in the trunk.

"I can't stand to see animals not receive a proper burial," he said as he climbed back into the car and restarted the engine. "We need to bury it. I'm going to take him home."

The discovery of the carcass had eradicated all signs of condescension from his features; his blue eyes were softly alert. "He's still warm," he said, during the drive home. "It must have happened just hours ago. The flies had already gotten to him, though."

Leena glanced at him with new curiosity. He parked in front of his small townhouse and opened the gate to the backyard for her. As he rummaged around for a shovel in the garage, she took his keys, which he'd dropped in the grass, and opened the trunk. She held her breath as she heaved the body into her arms and carried it to the back yard, struggling under ninety-plus pounds of dead weight. Draping the body over her knee, she settled into a lawn chair until Emerson returned from the garage, apparently unfazed at the sight of the corpse in her lap. He began digging, and after a few minutes she set the body on the grass and took the shovel from him. She could smell the decay on his hands and, moments later, on hers. They kept their heads bent somberly, as though mourning a shared pet, after shoveling dirt over the grave. Leena felt attached to the dead dog, attached to Emerson because he was a co-conspirator in their fabricated sadness.

Emerson dropped the shovel by the side of the fence and grabbed her arm. She followed him inside into the kitchen, where he turned on the faucet and washed the dirt off her hands, his freckled fingers rubbing her dark, callused ones. Then he guided her to the bedroom upstairs where he took off her clothes with great precision. He made love to her from behind on the bed, firmly grasping her waist. The sex, their first time together, was gritty; she was dry when he entered and bit the pillowcase to stop from screaming. She felt rear-ended, continually startled by the sensation of his body ramming into hers. After he came, breathing heavily into her neck, he glimpsed the wet stain of her saliva on the pillowcase and mistook it as a mark of ecstasy. He smiled slyly: "That poor, poor dog. But it sure got us going, didn't it?"

Leena collapsed onto her stomach, bending her head to smile at him, as his limp body drooped over hers. She turned over, grasping his face with both hands the way she believed a passionate lover would. White stretch marks traversed his stomach and thighs. As she traced the lines with her index finger, he confessed to being overweight as a child.

"Well, when I was little," she said, "I was ugly, and none of the boys would talk to me or touch me. So I pretended my pillows were men, and I'd try to seduce them. You can't even imagine the kinds of things I said to those pillows."

He laughed, and the gruff expulsion of noise surprised her. She rarely spoke about herself to anyone. At home, her conversations with her mother consisted of interrogations—suspicious questions from her mother and Leena's careful replies.

Later that evening he drove her home. He dropped her off three houses away from where she lived; she'd warned him about her mother on the first date. He asked her to lunch the next day, and she accepted.

"Well," he said as she opened the car door and stepped onto the curb. "I haven't had that much fun burying road kill with a woman in years."

"Most women are so high-maintenance these days," she said. "They want movies and dinners. Why can't they settle for a relaxing afternoon of burying dead animals?"

"You're funny," he said before driving away. Giddiness surged through Leena's body as she waved goodbye and walked over to her house.

Her stomach tensed as she opened the front door. She tiptoed across the marble entrance, sensitive to the noise of her black heels on the floor. Recently her mother had been following her. The day before, she'd opened her bathroom door to find her mother standing on the other side, asking to observe her feces as it would provide some insight into her seemingly perpetual status of old maid.

"You should let me take a look at your stool," her mother had said. "You need to pay attention to it. It tells you so much about your eating habits. If you continue to ignore it, you'll end up with a colon condition in less than a decade. And then it'll be even harder to find a husband willing to take care of you."

At her receptionist job at a law firm downtown, Leena received three or four emails a day from her mother containing information on new candidates for marriage from IndianHusbands.com, a website which guaranteed "A Matrimonial Candidate within five dates or less!" Her mother attached her own notes on the prospective husbands: *Gigantic belly, but has J.D. from Duke.* or *No hair on head, but plenty on arms and legs. Also, wants to get married immediately. Short waiting period.*

When Leena made it back to her bedroom, she went into the adjoining bathroom and scrubbed at the blush on her cheeks with soap and water. She changed out of her short black skirt and tank top into pink flannel pajamas. When she opened the bedroom door her mother was standing in the bedroom, her frail body wrapped in a thick black robe. Leena stepped back, startled. "Mom," Leena whispered, "what are you doing?"

At fifty eight, her mother was still a beautiful woman. Only her black, bitter eyes betrayed her immense fear of the world. "I suppose you went out with that white boy again," she said, scanning Leena's body for conspicuous signs of impropriety.

Leena sighed. "He works with computers. He's very successful."

"Career success isn't everything," her mother remarked. She carried a cup of freshly squeezed prune juice in her hand. "Here," she said, extending the cup to Leena, still surveying her for evidence of illicit behavior. "Drink this. It will make your bowel movements much more regular."

Leena downed the drink, wiping the excess juice from her chin with her hand. Her mother prattled on: "You're getting to the age where you need to marry. It's my dying wish that you end up with a good, kind Indian man. Your father would have wanted it. And I have a right to have grandchildren. After all the labor and the effort I put into raising you, I *deserve* grandchildren."

After Leena's father died of liver cancer, her mother ordained upon him, along with all deceased Indian relatives, the status of sainthood. She displayed pictures of him on the mantle, all taken during the first few months of the marriage. In them, her father's cheeks were still plump with optimism. They had not yet become recesses of rage and frustration.

"My group and I are having a meeting tomorrow," her mother continued, "and I would like you to attend. You've missed so many meetings that the other members are asking about you."

"You mean your gossip group?" Leena asked. Each Sunday, a group of middle-aged Indian widows who Leena referred to as the House of Un-Indian Activities came over for tea and samosas to rail against the evils of Houston society. They referred to themselves as INDIA—Indian-Americans against Needlessly Destructive Interracial Arrangements. Leena made it a point to confine herself to her room during these meetings, feigning debilitating diarrhea or a highly contagious case of the flu.

"It's no gossip group," her mother corrected her. "We've formed a very strong community. I expect you to be here at 3:00." She squeezed Leena's cheeks before disappearing into the blackness of the hall, an apparition in her ebony robe.

———

Emerson and Leena took a roundabout route to the restaurant for lunch the next day. She scanned the roads for corpses and spotted a mutilated, long-haired cat near Hermann Park. She'd come prepared, wearing a ratty sweater from her high school years over her long-sleeved shirt. They stopped by the side of the road. She was not queasy this time; she removed her sweater to wrap up the remains and placed the bundle of road kill in Emerson's back seat. After they'd buried the body in his back yard, Emerson placed a single hand on her shoulder, like a consoling husband.

They went inside after they finished, and Leena positioned herself seductively on the couch so that her short jean skirt rode up above her underwear. Emerson sank down beside her, grunted, and patted her behind absent-mindedly as he stood up again.

"Gotta get a beer," he said as he made his way to the kitchen.

"People say beer gives you big bellies," Leena called out from her place on the sofa. "But my dad, he drank at least three bottles of Shiner a day and stayed skinny. Other than his cheeks. They swelled up so much that I used to tell my mom that he had beer cheeks instead of a beer belly."

She waited, hoping that Emerson would place the beer back in the refrigerator and come back to the couch, resting his head on her thigh as he looked at her with a serious gaze. He'd inquire about her father's drinking: *What happened when your father drank? Does it bother you when I drink?* Slowly, he'd elicit responses from her—shy, tearful confessions—and he'd stroke her feet with the same tenderness he bestowed upon the road kill. *I've never told anyone about this,* she'd whisper between sobs, and he'd pull her into him. *They should have listened,* he'd say. *They all should have listened.*

Instead, he walked back into the room and popped the tab on the beer can as he sat down next to her. "That's cute," he said, "beer cheeks."

He finished off his beer, patting her thigh with no real urgency. She edged closer, stroking his leg and then moving upward to his groin, trying to remain discrete in her sexual overtures. He didn't respond until she began pulling at his underwear, at which point he summoned the sexual energy to kiss her.

They lay on floor after they finished, bodies disentangled.

"My father passed away a year ago," Leena said to him, after moments of silence. "My mother likes to think that he was a saint, even though they hardly spoke for a year before he died."

He didn't respond right away. "You're the first Indian girl I've ever dated. It's different, somehow, being with you. I don't know what to think of it."

Leena waited for more, but he lay motionless, in passive acceptance of the desperate succession of kisses she distributed over his translucent face. He began snoring mildly, and she stroked his hair, hoping that he would open his eyes and smile: *You've been here, waiting patiently the whole time?* He'd say. *You're an angel. An absolute angel.* He woke up a few minutes later, massaging his head into consciousness.

"I'm sorry about fading toward the end," he said as he showed her to the door. He shook his head. "Sex and beer just don't mix well."

Her stomach growled as she drove home. It was 2:30 in the afternoon, and the planned lunch had been derailed by the burial. When she slipped into her house, her hair was in disarray, and black and red make-up stains littered her face like graffiti.

Three middle-aged Indian women in saris were lounging in the living room around a coffee table full of samosas, Indian sweets, and cups of tea. Her mother, clothed in a muted gray sari, smiled at her and nodded toward an empty armchair completing the circle. Leena edged toward the table, murmuring vague apologies to the floor. She sat in the chair and crossed her legs, pulling her shirt down to cover her belly before realizing that this gesture of intended modesty enhanced her cleavage even more.

"This," her mother began, "is the third INDIA meeting. Indian-Americans against Needlessly Destructive Interracial Arrangements. INDIA!" She chanted, thrusting her fist into the air. The women repeated the chant, raising their fists and shaking them toward the ceiling. "Would anyone," her mother continued, "like to talk about their own experiences with interracial dating?"

Deepa began. Her daughter, she said, had been dating a white man for a month and had started wearing red saris for the first time in her life. She was elated that her daughter was finally embracing her culture before realizing that the boyfriend had a red sari fetish. "Now," Deepa said mournfully, "he comes over all the time, and they watch *Friends* and *ER* on my television. Then, they go to her bedroom, with her dressed in that red sari, and do God knows what."

Her mother nodded. "It is important for all of us to remember," she said with an air of contemplation, "that there are good, Indian men out there. We don't have to start dating white men who feed our insecurities."

The women nodded in Leena's direction, and she was suddenly aware that she was the target of an intervention. The women continued to lecture, and she sat very still, picking at the frayed ends of her skirt. When the women bleated "INDIA" at the end of the meeting, Leena raised a hesitant fist.

After everyone left, she helped her mother collect the tea cups and saucers. "The house seems so vacant after a party," her mother said. "It's full with people one moment, and then they rush out, and it's completely empty. It always unsettles me."

Leena set down the cups she'd gathered on a coffee table. "Mom, do you realize how embarrassing this was for me?"

"It was a friendly get-together," her mother said. "You need to have contact with more Indian women."

"They were talking to me like I was a coke addict. You need to stop pulling this crap."

Her mother's radar for impropriety was slightly defective; she could recognize an insult but could never target the precise offense. "Say please," she barked before leaving the room.

Leena retreated to her bedroom. As she stood in front of her dresser mirror, and her eyes fell on a box containing jewelry passed down to her from her father's mother. She opened the box and took out a heavy gold necklace and a bracelet embedded with red jewels. She fastened the necklace around her neck and the bracelet on her wrist. Her dresser was stacked with boxes of jewelry, her closet full of saris, and yet she had no idea how to put them to use. Every morning, she spent an hour eying the clothes in her closet, unsure of how to compose an outfit of American clothing and Indian jewelry, or a sari and high heels.

Her mother rarely wore Indian garb when Leena was growing up. Only after Leena's father died did her mother begin donning the saris around the house, insisting that their family had always been traditionally Indian. She chose to forget her husband's inclination to speak in a fake British accent around his co-workers, the fact that for years they'd slept in separate rooms, she in the study, he in the living room, neither in the bedroom that signified their union. She chose to forget the nights that Leena's father spent staring blankly at the television, his eyes growing more swollen with each beer he consumed.

Her mother was knocking on the door, and Leena opened it, accepting the prune juice her mother extended.

"That was rude earlier," her mother said. "I'm just trying to help you find a husband."

"I know," Leena said, tugging at the necklace.

"Your underwear was showing at the meeting," her mother said. "Your panties were bright red. Why would you wear fancy underwear unless you're trying to impress someone? I hope to God this isn't the case."

When Leena's father was alive, her mother prepared breakfast for her husband in an exquisite robe with her makeup flawlessly applied. One afternoon, when Leena was fourteen, she'd opened a bathroom door to find her mother naked in front of a full-length mirror, pinching a layer of fat on her stomach and surveying her body. When her mother saw Leena, she covered herself, but not before Leena had glimpsed the wetness of her eyes and the downward droop of her mouth. After that incident, Leena noted the distance between her mother and father when they sat on the couch together, the way her father awkwardly placed his arm around his wife in public, as though he'd never before touched her.

Leena drank the juice in a single gulp and handed the empty glass to her mother. The next morning, Leena found her discarded red underwear, along with her copy of Cosmopolitan magazine, stuffed in the kitchen trash.

———

Leena and Emerson put Carcass #3, the remains of a bunny, to rest on Monday evening. Huddling around the grave, Leena told him that he was her first. The lie surprised her, but she quickly justified it to herself; she had, after all, only been with four lovers before him, all one night stands, and remained a virgin in spirit.

"I couldn't help it," she said, lowering her eyes demurely to the ground. "I was planning on waiting until marriage, but I felt so connected to you that day."

Growing up, her mother engrained in her that pre-marital sex would lead to eternal spinsterhood. "A man who wants to marry you," her mother told her once, "will not accept a used woman." She expected a reaction of flattery and surprise: *Wow, you must have a natural knack for sex. I can't believe someone as beautiful as you waited for a dreg like me.*

But Emerson's shoulders sagged as he situated the mutilated rabbit in a sloppily dug grave. "That's a shame," he said. "I didn't know that. If I had known—" Leena brushed shoulders with him, nudging him to complete his sentence, but he wouldn't acquiesce, silently shoveling loose dirt over the corpse.

When he dropped her home, she sat in the car a moment longer, desperate to tell him she loved him, even as he dismissed her with a meager peck on the cheek.

———

Her mother was chopping cheese into meticulous squares when she entered the house. "My goodness," she gasped upon noticing Leena's shorts. "Do you want this white boy to rape you?"

She didn't answer and went to her bedroom, where she turned out all the lights and wrapped herself in a cocoon of sheets and blankets. She kept her face turned to the window as she heard her mother open the bedroom door.

Her mother perched on the bed, placing a hand on Leena's forehead. "Are you sick, baby?" she asked. "Is it a fever?"

She shook her head, and her mother collected her hair in her worn fingers. Leena closed her eyes, tilting her nose to the ceiling like a pet receiving much-needed affection.

Her mother braided her hair until Leena began to doze off. Between half-closed lids, she watched her mother curl up with a blanket on the floor next to her bed.

"You don't have to sleep here, mom," she murmured.

"Yes I do," her mother responded, wrapping her gaunt legs around a pillow. "No one so lonely should be alone. I'll stay with you tonight."

———

Carcass #4 was a possum on a kamikaze mission who had chosen the access road to Highway 59 as the venue for his suicide. It was a Tuesday night, and as they picked up the corpse Emerson spoke in terse commands: "Please hand me the bag." Then, later: "You need to hold the body with both hands."

The ride to his house was silent, and Leena chose her words carefully as she dug the grave. "When I was younger," she said, "I wanted to have my whole family buried in my backyard, so they would be close to me. After my dad died of liver failure, we had him cremated. I don't even know where my mother stored the ashes."

Emerson said nothing, and Leena pressed him: "Do you feel close to your dad?"

"We've grown apart," he answered. "You know how it goes. It's hard to stay in touch."

She waited for him to elaborate. He didn't. In bed together after the burial, his body remained limp and unresponsive despite her best efforts to arouse him.

"I'm sorry," he said, laughing nervously. "All that burying must have worn me out. My body isn't being very cooperative."

"We'll just keep trying," she said, stroking his groin. "It's okay."

He grabbed her arm. "It's not going to work," he said. "Trust me."

———

They found Carcass #5 late Wednesday evening. He was a chipmunk, the unfortunate victim of a hit-and-run. At the burial site, she told Emerson about her desperation to leave her home. "It's stifling there," she said. "My mother is so lonely, and she's obsessed with finding me an Indian husband."

He responded with a series of ambiguous "uh-huhs," and she kept talking, sharing the details of her parents' failed marriage—"My father stopped looking at my mother, much less talking to her. My mother kept trying to please him, but it never worked. It was awful to watch."

"He never told her he loved her," she continued. "Isn't that crazy? When people care about each other, they should say that."

Emerson was looking down at the disfigured chipmunk which they'd placed inside a plastic bag. "Poor thing," he said, placing the bag in the hole and piling loose dirt on top of the grave. "Torn to bits. Nothing's left of him."

They had sex in his car before he drove her home. The smell of death was still potent. Emerson climaxed quietly, and she compensated for his silence by moaning loudly as he finished. Half an hour later, he dropped her home without a word. She spent the rest of the night driving around her neighborhood, searching for a dead animal to warrant further conversation. But the streets and sidewalks were empty.

———

Emerson didn't call Thursday. On Friday, Leena took a longer route home after work, dawdling in particularly busy intersections where a disoriented animal would have little chance for survival. Later, she called the police department for information on high road kill statistics in the downtown Houston area, feigning horror at the number of carcasses she'd encountered in the Medical Center area: "I mean, is there anywhere else in the city with so many animals?"

Leena jogged around Hermann Park on Saturday hoping to stumble upon a newly deceased rodent. That evening, she dropped by a pet store: "What do you do with animals that die here?" she asked the baffled worker. More and more, she was discovering that the number of corpses in the Greater Houston area depended on abstract, variable factors: owner negligence, number of strays in the area, weather conditions.

Saturday night, Leena took out her prayer table from the closet, praying to God: "Please, please let me find a dead animal, somewhere." The next afternoon, she found an injured squirrel limping across Fannin. She thought of running over it but could not summon the courage to do it immediately. By the time she'd gathered the willpower, the squirrel had scurried away.

———

By the INDIA gathering on Sunday, Leena had found no further opportunity for connection with Emerson. She fidgeted as her mother lectured.

"There is no way," she said, "that you can avoid lapsing into a colonial relationship, the same kind that England had over India, where your intent is to constantly please your white partner. Leena, please listen to us and try to find someone who supports your culture."

Leena stared at the wall, her mouth rigid. When Leena was twelve years old, her mother and father began fighting about his frequent absence at night. Leena sat in her room with her ear against the door when she heard something smash against the wall. When she came out of her room, she looked at her mother, who was crouched on the living room floor with thin lines of blood on her neck from where the splinters of glass had struck her. Leena guided her mother to the bathroom, using wet toilet paper to wipe the wounds as her mother repeated: "He didn't mean it. Your father is a very good man. He's had a difficult time since we moved."

"A good man," her mother continued at the meeting. "That's all we want you to find, Leena. A good man who understands you, who respects your heritage."

"You're in a needlessly destructive interracial arrangement," she continued, leaning forward. "I only want you to be cared for."

"How much did it help you to marry an Indian man?" Leena asked.

Her mother began to speak and then stopped. She stared down at the floor. Leena regretted the words and sat mutely for the remainder of the meeting. She wondered whether all mothers chose to mentally erase the errors of their husbands or whether her mother was unique in this respect. The women raised their fists in the air at the end of the meeting, chanting: "INDIA! INDIA!" INDIA, she realized, was little more than an occasion for lonely women to gather together and share their collective pain.

At the end of the meeting Deepa handed Leena a flyer to a meeting for Indian Singles Galore. "A single pediatrician I know will be attending it," she whispered. "An ideal husband."

"Thank you so much," Leena said, "but I'm seeing someone right now."

"Oh?" Deepa asked, surprised. "Your mother never said anything. What does he do?"

Leena paused. *He buries dead animals.* "He works with computers. And conducts funeral services in his spare time."

"How strange," Deepa said. "What an odd combination."

The crowd of women dispersed, and after they'd left her mother was still sitting in her armchair, holding a samosa in one hand and a cup of tea in the other, her eyes vacant. Leena stood behind the chair, stroking her mother's hair. The strands were surprisingly light and brittle in Leena's hands. In spots, her hair stretched thinly over her scalp. Her mother seemed so sturdy, so determined, that Leena occasionally forgot her age. "I'm sorry," she whispered.

"It's okay," her mother said, her voice low. "I guess I've always had a fantasy that you would find the perfect Indian husband."

Leena glanced at the picture of her father on the mantle. It occurred to her for the first time that her mother had never fulfilled her own life-long dream of marrying the Good Indian Man.

———

On Monday, after work, Leena discovered the remains of an unfortunate pigeon on Elgin street. Most of the body had been swept away by drivers, but Leena placed a plastic bag over her hand and deposited what was left of the squashed body in a grocery bag. When she pulled up to Emerson's house, his blue Accord was parked by the curb.

She knocked, and he answered the door, taking the bag from her without a word. "This is all that was left of the bird," Leena said as Emerson carried the remains to the back yard. Leena trailed behind him. They stood on opposite sides of the soon-to-be grave, the corpse between them like a broken vow. As Emerson covered the corpse with dirt, Leena wondered how many animals Emerson had buried here over time. The dirt over the corpses was no longer loose but compressed over the soil, as though someone had ironed it out.

Emerson shook the dirt from his hands and began walking to the house. She stood still, aware that she could be a human tombstone to a body underneath. "I'm going home," she said. "But I wanted to say that I love you."

His face was passive when he looked up. "Youz don't know me."

She barely heard him. She thought of her father, too immersed in his own self-hatred to ever give love to another person. She thought of her mother, who spent thirty years tolerating her husband's emotional instability, hoping that he would declare his love for her. It was as though her father had a monopoly on love, and her mother was entirely at his mercy, powerless to claim it for herself.

She thought of the animals they'd buried that perhaps had never stood a chance in the strange mixture of rage and indifference in Houston. The overlooked, stiffened bodies littering the streets. The countless corpses that would remain unburied, left to the mercy of passing drivers. Bodies ripped apart by cars until lives were reduced to ambiguous stains on hard roads. They had nothing to mark their deaths, to testify to the fact that they'd ever lived. No one wrote their eulogies; no one mourned their deaths.

"I love you." She said it one last time, afraid that compassion, sensitivity, desire would crumble and fall from her body like dead leaves if she didn't speak them. Afraid that she, like her mother, would spend her life trying to extract love from another human being. The act of saying the words, though they remained unreciprocated, filled Leena with satisfaction as she left Emerson and his burial ground behind.

Zygomatic Arches

K. Goodkin

I. of evolution

near accident, these bones.
heft and shape.

trial, error, trial
error. the body betrays.

imperfect erect spine:
the valiant wielder of
skull pennant

II. of self

a compulsory burden to look into mirrors.
external structure, unified. tissue attached, hair
predictably sprouts from head,

when between the cheekbones, self
constructs. softball, pottery, tongue in
a stranger's ear.

III. of loss

humidity happens when memory meets water.
first a hiss, hotflash, steam. july, august, a graveyard
of occupied windows, wicker chair stoops, yellowing spider
plants. a long gone body sweatpressed against.
when august meets september. migration.

Bright Black

Theodore Rigby

Sketches of Next Summer

Adam O. Davis

1.

I was in the garden with my metal detector
when I heard a muffled ring beneath my feet.
I dug and found a telephone, dirt-encrusted

and ringing, and brushed off the receiver.
A voice asked me how I found the phone
and I told him. Was it hard to hear, he asked.

Not on a quiet day, I replied. She must have
been ignoring me all these years, he said.
I'm sorry to bother you. I won't call again.

2.

An early hour in which I notice dogs
      lounging on the lawn like sphinxes; also sprinkler chatter,
the chirping of sunfed bugs. Some soundtrack
      to paranoia putters in the basement, chained.

A later hour in which I wonder:
      Why are shoes fashioned from the shoeless?
It's an odd thought, but not as odd as others
      that might arrive later from latent minds.

3.

The landscape is a skillet of coffee shops,

every waitress named for a gemstone.

4.

Soused, she couldn't suss the rhythm

and the night roared on in its flammable way
while she wept upon the windowpane.

What next? Only hours before she held

him and swore an oath to detachment. Now lost,
her stomach was empty as a lunchbox, her heart

bleated from within its zippered case.

5.

In the park, a door in the statue
opened and three people in Victorian dress

exited. They looked around uneasily
at the sunbathers who took notice,

the startled chainsaw juggler's audience.

"This won't do," said the woman
with a whalebone umbrella. "This won't do

at all." They returned into the statue

and the door shut behind them.
For a moment after there was the question

of whether things should continue

as they had been before the intrusion,
whether to spoil the day with comment.

But the juggler paid little attention, counting

each finger of each hand until he was satisfied
to have escaped the scene unscathed,

then collected his armory and left.

6.

The heat, enough to crack glass,
dried gutters to old testament gulches
and there was violence in everyone.

7.

The bees built their hive until the hex
was held in honeycomb, hidden from us
in their headache machine. We waited,
so certain of damnation we didn't notice
the season carried on without us, leaving
us forever stranded in the solstice.

8.

There's so little I'm scared of now.
But still so many ways for fear to find
you and even more methods for love.

9.

On the corner, that house we watched
burn down is filled with birds and bits

of burnt furniture. We toss coins
into the wreckage for good luck, carve

our names into the blackened trees
that surround it for ceremony.

It's later than you think. Already I can feel
the Earth shifting its axis, bearing us back

toward winter. I could walk all night.
We should walk all night.

from 1001 Sentences

Tony Tost

A vast Orphic needle runs through my flesh, answering up from each point of entry—my poetics is that of a willful promiscuity. My singing a kind of swallowing, my swallowing a kind of singing. A real sentence can be just as instructive as ones that have already been written. The goal is to situate Eros in this time and place. Sentience, drop after drop of it—whether it be of whales or letters or men—is the basic soup of astonishment. The outward is a bride. And it is by the birth of the will that the words can be seen and thought of by sewing them together on the head of a pin. Each sentence signifies the tension between the past and future of the poem; this is why every sentence must perpetually be prepared to destroy itself. The brim of my poet's hat appears to determine and outline the expanses of my vision, suggests the identities I will carry with me beyond each grave. Here I am, talking to my angels, sighing before the wavelengths; the Mozart of mistakes.

To respect an accident is to respect the world of facts.
When I finally made it out of the woods I hitchhiked back
to Missouri that very night so I could go ahead and have his
baby, etc. Sentimentality is one more instrument for
innovation. The sun has pierced an angel—one who, in
her terror, has gnawed at the very hammer (the blood on it)
that is currently in my possession; hereby, the sun is quite
capable of beholding each of these very moments, through
my eyes. One advantage of fragmenting the present self in
this way is that all these sentences can eventually be seen
as the remote biological past. Mine is the body of a living
individual, a poetic accompaniment: maintains a distance
between images and the processes used in obtaining them.
Swans peck at the heads of angels, each transported into
perfected bliss. I know of no conquest sweeter than that of
the will over imagination, the exaltation of unaccountable
forms. The angels rise again, play their hunches, reach
down and merge into belief. It is in a wish for moral
splendor that they medicate the emotional atmosphere,
color our given situation as mysterious and suddenly
expressed.

Your thousand and one years of intense celestial contact are now but an object for nostalgia; the miracle of nostalgia is that it conjures precise objects even in its search for an unyielding, inaccurate emotional field in which an identity may become as untouchable as it is unreal. My destiny is bigger than yours. Gunnar Olsson writes, "It is in the crevice between convention and deviance that language becomes erotic." On the back of my paycheck I am writing history. The professor claims victory, raising his hoof. A desire for sexual contact condenses inside me, trickles out as a gesture, drifts: nostalgic, hegemonic, understood. A maestro is able to demonstrate his or her power in just a handful of notes. Weeping should be considered an intellectual activity. I fucked the fucking river. This is Ezra Pound's famous haiku.

Another True Love Story

Andrew Touhy

> *"My son, be warned!"*
> —*Daedalus*

Somehow, the poor fly's heart was replaced with an old Honda engine. You would think he couldn't have flown in this condition, but flies, like ants and spiders and many other insects, have immeasurably strong, remarkably light-weight exoskeletons. And anyway look at airplanes, helicopters, and space shuttles. The fly's real problem was flying too fast. No way could his tiny, webbed wings beat as many times per second as the engine demanded at full throttle; and the engine was always open full-throttle because the fly was desperately in love.

Now flies only live on average twenty days or so (most humans, and even most flies, are unaware of this), and our fly too is unaware of this because the lover he's looking for, who stole his heart the first time, died weeks ago. Our poor fly would be dead too, if it weren't for the transplant, but that's another story altogether. The story here is the fly, who is furiously beating his two tiny wings at such a rapid clip, all in a vain attempt to find someone who is long gone, or never existed but in the Ideal, or was just flirting for sport or sowing her wild oats before agreeing to a loveless marriage with a decidedly older (though not wholly unattractive) fly with a Tahoe lake house…which is, come to think of it, a sad and horrible story. One that, really, can only end badly for all parties involved: heart-wrenching disappointment on the part of the lovesick fly, not to mention a lot of huffing and puffing when the poor thing finally tires out and begins his flaming, Icarus-like plunge to the ocean below. A too-comfortable, hollowing existence for the bride-to-be fly. Alzheimer's, or its equivalent, for the geriatric fly.

And these days, with all that's going wrong in the world, we sure don't need to read Underdog stories, or Cinderella stories, or Little-Engines-That-Could or whatever stories with heroes dropping to their certain, depressing deaths. Something like that's just plain bad for morale, no matter what kind of insect or animal or human being. So let's instead take a moment here to marvel at this steadfast fly in flight. Black speck—less than that, to treat both perspective and the magnitude of the fly's achievement fairly—zipping and buzzing across a cloudless sky of royal blue; laboring, yes, a little, smoking some, sure, but bearing the weight of that engine (and, of course, true love) with all the rebellious pluck and casual magnificence of the god those up-ward-gazing fishermen, ploughmen, and shepherds might mistake him for.

———

No, even that's a mistake. *Everything* I've told you so far has been a mistake. Let me begin again:

An old Honda engine, somehow, awoke in the body of a fly. He awoke shocked and saddened but trembling with longing. And he's driving the fly, desperately driving the fly, and won't stop (sorry, poor fly) until he finds the old Honda to which he'd always belonged, and loved with a passion unparalleled in the history of man, beast, or machine. Which is, for that matter, another love story all together.

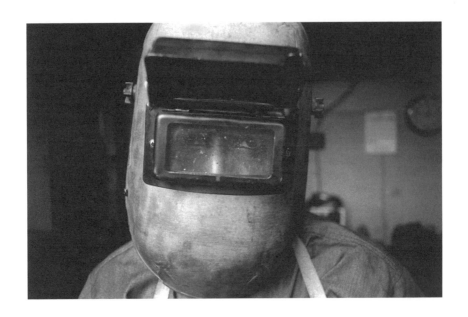

Wali

———

Theodore Rigby
from *Migrant Workers in South Korea*

Etymological Divagation

Jasper Bernes

I like the part in your movie where evil—related to *up,* to *over*—is only suffering with escape velocity, an excess, cumbrous as refinanced virginity at the end of holding self to its selfsame retirement plan. My son cries for three hours straight. We do not have an understanding about this. There is a rain of certainty in the garden and a big thaw tumbling from his body all prehistory and verticals. There are extra parts which we *do* bury in the sky, which, having exceeded all estimates of the distance of the planets from their magnetic discharges in the temperate parts of the world, return as a taste for veal, a leafy veil of spatial disturbances around a coaxial node. For example, under the column marked *yours,* it turns out that the yacht, which was not, as had been thought, Hitler's yacht, donated by a restaurateur with a colorfully impertinent past, and sunk ceremoniously and with great but non-specific meaning nearly two miles from the officially sanctioned and notarized spot, has to get hauled up and re-sunk where it can form an artificial reef without endangering commercial ship traffic. Under the column marked *mine,* a holiday's greeting from an old friend in the form of a subpoena. I buy a special pen that can write underwater, but only in verbs, which is too bad, because you were hoping to talk about how punishment actually precedes pain in Latin, and how that explains everyone's pretending that everyone else's misery is not their fault, which it isn't really, just invisible. It pokes out the devil's eyes, for like two seconds, thinking this. Terrible, and terribly enlarged concepts, in graffiti written underwater— by people with, I suppose, hightech gear—all over the barnacled *Ostwind.*

from Figures for a Darkroom Voice

Noah Eli Gordon and *Joshua Marie Wilkinson*

The signal is two women standing side by side before the elephant door. Each time one of them speaks another metric layer of sawdust pours up from the earth. Their teeth, winter; their hands, gauze; eyes, little lions; their jewels, jewels. If a tree asks to be cut into a casket while a man dreams of sawblades from his skinny hospital bed, then the nameless boy's uncanny forgetfulness constellates a swarm of incorrect light. Who says pleasure means you have been weaned too early for your own good? Our private animals are not guardians of tenderness. Water bristles into snowy radio wires, until the pigeon boys ready their pencils, draw a train tunnel onto the kitchen wall like a huge mouse hole. Is this a part for touching or a touching part? The last car on the last train like a tinted memory carves a new set of tracks.

Stars are no map of civility in our garden of little let-downs

———

recall the one anecdote in your inkblotter

———

& three geldings pound a sky-scape
into a lesson in meteorology.

Here's the mechanical garden with its watery flowers & sparks. Here's the bull's hoof cast in something like iron, leaving footprints in the shape of broken clouds. Here's a dresser carved from bone. & here, inside of it, is its good cocaine scent asking you to punish the parts of yourself closest to the piano in construction, furthest from persistent woods in each fairytale that propels us to misrecognition. If you enter them do so with a year's worth of butcher birds to seal your steps up in the muck.

Goodbye, subtle inventory of where what I have to say goodnight with

is this the button-breaking ice wind's wooden-crossbeam rattle

———

a bag of red lemons

a boy hammering through radio static

———

Who wouldn't want a twin to enter the gates with?

The Atlas Complex

e. bojnowski

1 /   the hills are batter
scouring our heads until moist
with birth
its womb held me in like it was growing crystals
born with a target upon my head
drew milk from my bones as we
slept in the crook of its neck
a wounded dove
she will forever drag her fingers along the washboard as
the sun puts out a searchlight
he tucks them into the folds of his jeans
so they will not sunburn
sticking straws in her eyes sucking out her vision
smiling like a plaid shirt
as they collect rage on plastic window blinds
their sex stabbing the gray sky
clenching butter in their fists
they rape every rain drop

2 /   you love me in my sarcophagus
murdering wool
gluing carpets to our feet
(the candles will not invite her for dinner)
the roof of his mouth made of cotton plant
soaking up her tongue's angst
they walk through claws
shoving flowers down their throats

remember how they murdered her pillow

the urban lull of the earth below

making the stars flinch

they shove wind down my esophagus

my skin bloats with the weight of monsoon and it stretches, a new
elder

the loose wires growing from my head dragging behind me

collecting forest floor trash-

a crook tripping line

this raw daylight chewing on it like gum

if i could only crawl back in

3 /   we have flat shadows

she died with their marrow in her

her fingers are convinced they will become trees and stretch

far from here piercing the mother in the hallway and the neighbors

huddled by a mailbox

the holes smoking like barbeque pits

the mist of tears hangs down like savage moss

the air thick with past heat

strangling the wind with our shackles

fed them rubber shoe soles and

angry doorknobs

our organs glowing from the alleys

placing acorns on our fingers

tapping them across horizons

the ideal knives would have finished me off but

we are older than our own teeth

Of a Bullet's Clarity

Jeffrey Douglas

This all started with a note.

> PIZZA MAN,
> IF I DON'T ANSWER, COME INSIDE, GO TO THE ROOM
> AT THE END OF THE HALL. IF I DON'T ANSWER, I'M
> WORKING. JUST COME IN.

The letter flaps on the door, ignorant of its own meaning, like a naked child in a room of adults. With the pizza box hot and moist on my hand, Mehul's warning chops through my head in his broken, Indian English:

"Never go inside."

Tip money is what turned the door, why I went in.

The house has all kinds of hanging paintings, with no real furniture except for a few vases on some pedestals and a TV with a smashed-in screen. In the TV there's all kinds of broken glass and some tubes and stuff, and then a picture of a starving African kid with a fly for a teardrop.

A plaque on the TV reads REALITY SHOW.

I figure it's some kind of artist's run-down house by the time I reach the back room. By the time I knock on the door a few times, I wonder if the artist is even home.

I knock again. Wait.

Nothing.

I push the door in to warm air and a smell of something musty, something sweet. I cringe because there's red dots everywhere, red flecks, beautiful drops all over the white walls.

There are tables around the room, a bunch of half-painted canvases, another TV, and a guy in a computer chair in the middle of the room with his head back.

The flecks belong to the guy's head, the hole in it looking at me. I can see right through his skull, to the red spray scattered on a half-finished canvas of a naked woman looking at a sketched sunset.

The pistol on the floor, below his dangling right hand, has a mischievous red haze on its strong chrome.

"Jesus," I say, realizing how quiet it is sharing a room with a dead guy. My words bounce around, bounce around without disturbing the meridian of colors, and blood, and silence, and hot, and smell of double-vegetarian thin crust.

"Lucifer," I say.

I wonder if the cops are going to question me. Are going to think I did it.

That's when I see the tape in the mouth of the VCR labeled PUSH.

"Fucking cliché!" I say. "A dead artist with a tape to push in." His final explanation of why he killed himself, of what this miserable world did to his tortured soul.

I look at the hole gaping his face, his nose crunched in and glistening purple, bloody strings loose, dripping from his slack lips.

I walk over to the tape and push it. It fuzzes; I take out the pizza, open the box, and take out a slice.

The guy fuzzes onto the screen, his slender face, intense eyes, short brown hair, the pinnacle artist trying too hard to sound intelligent.

The pizza's still hot.

This suicide artist, this intense guy trying too hard to be well spoken, looks at the camera and starts.

"Soto," he says in a harsh premeditated sense, "this whole thing started with you saying you loved me..."

"Cliché!" Pizza bits out of my mouth.

"...I'd never be the amount of an animal you measure to deserve, and accept as a life partner..."

"Shut the fuck up!" A bell pepper falls from my mouth to the bloody carpet.

So he goes on for a while about this Soto girl, and how great she is and how worthless he is, and says some stuff about the deforming cruel hands of Time that sound like they should be important to someone but mean nothing to me, and then says, "So, you see, I had to end myself so you'd find me, in a moment of perfect splendor, as you know, as we discussed. So when you find me, stand in the room and be the one to announce to the world that I'm dead, that I've passed on this remorseless shell of a human." He bunny-mark-quotations the word *human*. "It's important that you've found me, as we discussed, as my moment in death will mean something I never could have meant to you in life."

I smell cigarettes.

"You weren't," she says in the doorway, "supposed to be the one to find him, Pizza Man."

The first thing I notice are the enormous brown glasses, curved and dark, wrapping around her eyes, looking like car headlights. The next thing, these deep red tattoos swirling down her arms, muscle sinew inked onto her pale skin. Her face is small and sharp, her waist is thin, dark hair frames her face in these thin crescents.

The cigarette burns bright to her inhale.

"Soto?" I ask.

She exhales a patch of hazy skulls and nods.

"This your boyfriend?" I ask.

"Not exactly," she says.

She moves quickly to him, her movement all hips, light steps, and all hips. She leans in close to what was his face. "Neat."

She turns the computer chair around; it squeaks. She looks at the flecks and runs her fingers through pools of blood, brings a drop to her lips.

"I'm sorry," I say. "I think I missed something."

She looks up at me, those dark headlights, she blows out smoke. "You handled it well, Pizza Man."

At this point, I don't feel as disturbed as I feel I should. I think above all else, that disturbs me the most.

The pistol below his dangle of fingers hazed in red.

"I'll be calling." She throws her head back, flicks her crescent bangs and walks out, all hips, light steps, and those skinny hips.

So I'm left there, with a half-eaten pizza, Hole Head, a visit from a vampire, a suicide video, all appearantly unintended for me.

The police and their flashing lights and fast questions and probing responses and strict mannerisms believe my story at about 11 o'clock that night.

Mehul doesn't believe me. He wants to fire me.

It's the next day standing at the back door, the one leading from the alley. I explain, "It wasn't my fault, Mehul, c'mon, this guy commits suicide and you fire me?"

"I have deliver all orders yesterday." He slides his hand out vertically. "All myself, no help, not even wife."

He stands there with his beer, and that intense Indian eye. It's 11 o'clock and the sun is high.

"I was with the cops."

He drinks his beer.

"What do you want me to do?" I ask.

"You tell them," he says, "you have work, they talk to you later. In my country that works."

"It's different out here, Mehul."

Just then the phone rings. Mehul stands there looking at me, holding his beer, like he's deciding to hang me or cut my throat.

"C'mon, Mehul."

He drinks his beer.

The phone keeps ringing.

"Okay, you make this one, and I think about it."

The inside of the shop has this dirty cement ground, with dingy steel tables and big ovens and dough makers and sinks, and this perpetual floury smell of recycled pizza sauce and dough and cold pepperonis.

I lean against the counters. Mehul doesn't let me sit unless I clean something, and I don't like to clean, so I stand. I work the rest of that day with Mehul over me like a storm crow, waiting for him to tell me to leave.

I made forty-seven dollars in tips, enough to pay my phone bill and sleep that night like I did the night before, thinking of blood-tasting Soto and Hole-in-His-Head. Staring at the ceiling trying to come to terms with the fact I found this guy dead, and ate some pizza. That I saw this girl lick his blood, shake her hips, and all my humanity could muster was whether the cops would pin me or not.

The lack of it disturbing me disturbs me the most.

So the next day, after barely sleeping, I get to the pizza shop and there's a lady in a skirt suit, a scruffy cameraman with a backwards hat, and a chubby guy with a long microphone, glasses, and a double chin.

They're out there talking to Mehul, the lady with the microphone in Mehul's fake smile. The big microphone hanging over him, the camera trained on his leathery, tanned face in the morning sun.

"Ah!" Mehul sees me. "Here's my best employee now."

He shakes my hand and pats my shoulder.

The mic in my face, the big mic above me, the camera trained on me. The lady smiles wide like someone desperate for you to overlook how uncomfortable they make you.

"Gloria Estellas, Channel 7 News," she says with a too-many-toothed grin wrapped in red lips. She smells strong.

"Yeah, I know," I say.

Too strong.

"You're a smart kid, Finnegan Mihelich. How old are you?"

It's a wave of smell asking me questions.

"Twenty-one," I say.

She looks at the camera, on the street in front of the pizza shop, smiles, and says, "We're with the alleged suicide Pizza Man, twenty-one-year-old

Finnegan Mihelich." She turns to me. "Tell me, Finn...I can call you Finn, right?"

"I don't care."

"Tell me, Finn. How did you feel when you found cult artist thirty-four-year-old Leland Harland dead in his studio?"

"I don't know," I say, at the bottom of anything else to tell her. "Not much."

"Interesting," she says.

And that went on for another ten minutes with me not saying much, and Mehul jumping in to say things like, "I hired and trained him myself at Pizza Man on Carson Street," then smiling into the camera.

After they leave, in the shop, Mehul offers me a beer and says, "Sit, sit."

He says, "You make delivery today and tomorrow?" with his intense flash smile.

"I thought Rocko was delivering tomorrow?"

"No, no, he's not good as you, you deliver tomorrow."

I shrug. The phone rings.

It's a Friday, so the phone starts ringing more and more and more.

Regular deliveries, five and ten dollar tips, wasting gas money Mehul doesn't reimburse me for, but feeling like I'm not at work because I'm listening to my own music.

Then, 3929 Gainhill.

The pizza box is hot and warm on my palm. Standing on the porch, it's 8:47 with a smell of mushrooms and bell peppers.

There's a metal plaque on the door, bathed in porch light reading KNOCK HARD, HARD OF HEARING.

So, I knock hard, and the unlocked, unlatched door creaks open to a white-walled entrance with tan carpet. There's a small card table in the little entranceway with car keys, a cell phone charger, and two wrinkled twenties on a stack of unopened envelopes.

I knock on the door harder, and wait, looking at the green bills to be broken to tip money.

Knock harder.

I have change in my pocket, so I can break the twenties, leave the change, take five dollars for myself, a modest cut, leave the pizza to the old people or disabled folks or whatever, no one hurt.

Walk in to set the pizzas on the card table, and in the living room to the left, two people sit on the couch with glistening red things coming out of their necks.

"Shit!" I almost drop the pizza.

There's blood down their necks and onto their clothes and couch and carpet, and the things coming out are swollen cartilage of their jugulars.

The knives on the floor, angular steel, dressed in liquid red.

I walk over and there's angled canvases leaning up against the couches between their open legs. Their faces, by the way, are almost content, had their lives not slipped away a few hours ago. One guy's Asian, with a shaved, wide, round head and a goatee. The other guy's white with thin black hair past his ears, big eyebrows, and a skinny neck. Well, a skinny, slit, bloody neck.

Anyway, these canvases between their legs, one has REALITY written on the bottom, the other one has SHOW. But the thing is, their blood leaked in probing red tentacles over the white canvas surface. From their slit throats, down their clothes' curves, creeping down to the canvases, their throats came down to drip over the words in this disturbing brand of what I wouldn't call "art" so much as I would call dripping blood.

There's the TV and VCR, with the PUSH ME tape.

"Fuckin' unoriginals," I say.

Ralph Waldo cruises through my head, but I don't say it.

There's blood squishing in the carpet where I step over to the VCR and push the tape in, sit down, and open the pizza box. The TV comes on. The image of these two dead guys, when they were alive at least, fuzzes onto the screen and they start:

"This all started with," the Asian Guy says with a voice hushing exhausted excitement, "as I'm sure you know, the artist Leland Harland."

"The late, great Leland Harland," adds the skinny white guy.

Asian guy says, "And to make our mark in the group, the intellectual bloom of our modern society trap..."

"Fuck your group!" Pizza chunks falling out, "You're dead!"

"…We feel it vital to spite time, to defy the deforming hand of decline that is time," Asian Guy says.

"To take the ticks on the wall into our own hands," Skinny Guy says.

"Gimme a break," I say.

"You've stumbled," she says from the doorway, "onto something you probably don't want to, Pizza Man."

I don't need to look to see her in the doorway, dark headlights, trailing cigarette smoke, red sinew tattoos curling her pale arms. Those hips.

"Your 'not-exactly-boyfriend' wasn't the only one?" I ask.

Asian Guy says, "To wait around for death isn't as clarifying an existence as taking one's life. Elegance is in a life given, not taken."

"Uh," Soto moans, and I'm drawn to the pleasure in the swivel in her hips. "Such truth," she says.

I look at her, then the screen, then back at her. Swallow pizza and say, "You buy that shit?"

She comes into the room, all rhythm of hips.

"It's the truth, isn't it," she says, taking pictures of Dead Guys with a small silver camera. "These aren't depressed suicides missing the sun or miserable with life, Pizza Man." She gets the camera close to the swollen jugular of Asian Guy. "Having the title of 'President' doesn't make you one."

I bite pizza, look at her, and say, "Sure it does."

Waving her hand, she says, "What's important is them, in their ultimate state of weakness and perfection."

"As Leland Harland would say," White Guy spouts on the screen, his voice excited and pitched near breathless, "'leave behind a hideous corpse and a beautiful body of work'."

"Ahhh!" Soto moans loud. "Such sharp truth."

The cops with their flashing lights keep me longer with their clipped, gruff questions, and I thought they really figured me a part of all this. I just kept explaining my story and finally got home at four that morning.

My apartment is cement floors with rugs we laid down, wood chairs in the living room, a broken pinball machine, a lone refrigerator that buzzes louder than something really loud, and four roommates in two bedrooms. I made seventy-eight dollars, pooled the rest of my tips from the week and left all I had, one hundred and eighty-two dollars, on the table with a note reading, SOMEONE SPOT ME THE OTHER 18. I'LL PAY YOU BACK IN BEER, –REALITY SHOW.

Dave's snoring again, and I lie on my mattress with an old itchy blanket, squeeze my pillowcases stuffed with dirty shirts and socks, and lie there wondering about dead guys.

The ceiling is dark, but it seems to form a face, a confused and wondering Asian face, blank eyes and an ugly, bald head.

I look at it and don't feel much except cold.

"Leave behind a hideous corpse…"

It still disturbs me I'm not more disturbed by all this.

"…and a beautiful body of work."

Next day, the camera crews more than triple.

Mehul is outside with about seven microphones jammed in his leathery, tan face. His hair slicked and combed to the side, his shirt pressed and the top three buttons open to show his hairy chest. His gold chain loops down, glinting in the early afternoon.

"There he is!" someone says.

"Ah," Mehul shouts, "my favorite, my best employee."

Microphones in my face, strong smells of too many toothed smiles, words blending together.

"Do you know any of these people?"

Their look reminds me of jackals around a big, bulky animal in Africa.

"Do you find death repulsive?"

I'm surrounded and near feeling violated.

"Ever wonder why you?"

"Have you ever contemplated suicide?"

"Does pop culture have anything to do with these deaths?"

Mehul pushes his way over, puts his arm around me, pats my back, and poses with a smile.

"Does anyone ever ask you to kill them?"

"How do you get in the house?"

"Shoot them?"

"Is the door unlocked?"

Mehul starts pushing me toward the door of the shop.

"Please, please!" he calls out, pushing people out of the way. "We talk later, much work to do, much work here at Pizza Man on Carson Street," he flashes a smile at the cameras.

We get to the shop door, and he opens it and pushes me through. Solidarity and the perpetual smell of floury pizza sauce and cold pepperonis and shredded mozzarella in every corner I've never been able to get the broom around.

The phone's already ringing.

Mehul locks the door and comes behind the counter.

"Sit, sit, sit," he says. I sit. He runs to the back, comes back with two beers.

He opens one and hands it to me. It's cold and good.

"Okay," he says. "We tell them I send you to crazy people." His smile is all yellow teeth.

"Why?" The next drink is better than the first.

"You don't see money?" He gestures to the phone.

Rent was eighteen dollars short.

The phone is still ringing.

"If we try to make it intentional," I say, "it won't have as much interest, we'll just be doing something we meant to."

He looks confused.

The backup phone line starts ringing.

"But if we make it look like this is just a place suicides call up to find them dead," I say, swirling my finger around the can's ridge, "then people can't help but be interested."

Mehul sips his beer.

I guzzle mine down to an empty can.

The third phone line rings.

"Okay," he nods, "we tell them first was accident, but after second, I can tell crazy people, and I send my best employee to see." His grin seems to be filling with more teeth, more sharp teeth.

"All things considered, Mehul, you only ever have one employee delivering."

"So?"

I shrug. "Fair enough."

"Okay," he rushes over to the phones, all four of them ringing now.

Now it all really starts getting odd. Add a dead artist to your life and you're an instant celebrity. Sometimes my deliveries would back up three hours. People didn't care. It wasn't about the pizza. Mehul made me park in front. For deliveries, I'd have to wade through photographers and camera crews, blurred words and microphones jammed, shoved, shot at me.

It wasn't about pizza.

I'd show up, knock, and it would mostly open to goth kids, greasers, or punkers who want to see the Suicide Pizza Man.

"Aww, you're that guy on TV," the skinny kid with the cut-off black shirt and spiked Mohawk says, handing me twenty dollars for an eight-dollar pizza. "Right on."

"Wanna come to my room?" the little goth girl with black and purple hair, black eyeliner, and pale skin asks. I tell her I have more deliveries, she gives me her phone number, a ten-dollar tip, and in the car I put her number with the rest.

"Aww, Jimmy, check it out." A riled group of greasers with slick pompadours, Dickies jackets, and wallet chains. They shake my hand rough, pat me on the back, and say, "This guy's nuts, man, can we get a picture?" I pose there with them on the porch, in my Pizza Man shirt, hat, and red square box. They shake my hand again and ask, "Are you on MySpace?" I shake my head, and between the six of them, they give me seventy-nine dollars and seven cents for a twenty-six-dollar bill.

A lot of middle-aged women and older men. The women hug me, have me sign something, sometimes apologize for me having to see that, then tip, and tip well. Old guys always want to tell me about the time their friend's legs were blown off in some distant country a long time ago. The longer I listened, the more they tipped. I felt like a dolphin doing tricks on command, a well-fed dolphin.

The one that got the FCC involved was the backyard fence, open, with loud techno music coming from back there. I go back expecting a party and find this girl at a wood table in the flat grass back yard, facedown in a big bowl of vomit. There's blue and white lights strung up around the table, and on it is a stereo I switch off, and a big empty pill bottle on its side.

It looks like there was more vomit or something in the bowl before she threw up and drowned in it, but I distinctly see bits of noodles and rice and some vegetables, chewed and half digested. Around the bowl is written, REALITY SHOW, and, TOXIC SLUDGE FOR YOU TYRANTS TO PLUNGE THE INNOCENT ALABASTER OF THE WORLD INTO YOU EMOTIONLESS, INHUMAN ROBOTS!

On the back of her shirt it says, INNOCENT ALABASTER OF INFANTS AND THE HUMBLE.

Disturbed at my lack of disturbance, yes, but now more disturbed at how many dollar signs I see. This is good for business.

Over in the corner of the backyard is the VCR and TV. And tape reading PUSH ME.

I shake my head. "Still unoriginal."

I look around quickly and catch a glimpse of Soto peeking from behind the garage fumbling with her lighter.

"See you!" I say, turning around. "Come out and say some abstract, enigmatic shit."

She walks out, all hips, like she wasn't going to say something behind me for her grand, mysterious entrance.

"So," she says.

She starts taking pictures of Drowned Girl.

"The fuck is this Reality Show?" I ask sitting on the table. The vomit doesn't smell like alcohol vomit, the kind I'm used to. It smells sweet, like spilled hot chocolate.

She snaps another picture, then slides out a cigarette.

"You haven't figured out yet?" She flicks a lighter and holds the flame to the end and it burns bright to her inhale.

"I'm sorry, I just find them as cold meat." I point at her. "And you're always leaving me for the cops to explain."

She smiles and giggles. "You're doing well." She looks at me and lowers her glasses, her eyes a subtle green, kind of a letdown, really. I thought the eyes behind those glasses would pierce like bullets, but they don't. "I can tell," she says sliding them back up.

I say, "Yeah, I'm doing fine, this stuff doesn't bother me all that much…"

She giggles, wiggling her hips.

"...I just don't see why these people are so quick to die," I say, picking up the pill bottle, "so fast to end themselves."

She flicks her cigarette and takes more pictures, the red curling sinew of her frail, strong arms curtailing her movements.

"I think you do," she says. "Like I said, I can tell."

I look up at the sky. It's big and endless and a waning dirty gray and orange in the sunset. "Wait, is that what you meant?"

She lights another cigarette and walks out of the backyard.

Watching those hips, I want to follow, the sway of her arms, I want to see where she goes. I look back at Drowned Girl, her sitting there facedown in that stuff, floating tendrils of her brown hair.

The cops don't question me too much. This one wasn't necessarily a suicide I could have caused. Pills don't speak with the clarity of a bullet, the simplicity of a blade.

After that, the FCC links a help line to our phone. Mehul was instructed if the customer seems a little frantic he was to transfer them to a hot line of waiting specialists.

"I never transfer them, okay?" Mehul says after the FCC guys leave. "Bad for business, too bad for them."

They even made a newly graduated psychiatrist, Dr. Grayber, come sit with us a few nights out of the week. Every fourth call, Dr. Grayber gets on the phone and asks when the last time the customer smiled was. Dr. Grayber was young, but his head was already bald and graying. He had thin shoulders, beady, scrutinizing eyes, and glasses. He was pretty cool, but we couldn't drink beer around him, and with as much beer as Mehul had been giving me lately, I really didn't like Dr. Grayber around.

"Okay," he'd say slowly, methodically, with a voice like dripping honey. "Is there anything inside of you that's angry, or does there seem to be something missing?"

I'd always wish for speakerphone, to hear regular customers say, "Yes, something is missing, food."

Amateur suicides started calling, too. I'm not sure how you have an amateur suicide, considering if you kill yourself, you're dead, but they lacked the class and artistic value of Reality Show suicides. These were the unmotivated, unoriginal suicides who still put notes on the door.

> DEAR PIZZA MAN,
> COME IN, THE DOOR'S UNLOCKED.

I stopped trusting letters after the first. Every time I'd get a letter, I'd call the cops, they'd come out, and sure enough there'd be a corpse in there, shot, or slit, or something, but no canvases or beautiful body of work. Just a hideous corpse. No Soto either. I'd always look around for her trying to sneak up on me.

The cops let me check out some of the more random ones. They were starting to think of me as some kind of celebrity, too. The best was this one guy, head in the oven with a sign on his back that said NO FUNERAL. Apparantly suicide cases are cops' "busy work," excuses to drink coffee, hang around, and wait for coroners. They liked me 'cause of that.

This was good for business, great for my image with the police, but not very good for me lying awake at night. This was all rent money, and people honking at me on the street, and piling dead bodies. Nine by now. I was being more appreciated at the doorstep than regularly. I was a traveling celebrity spectacle, a celebrity call service, a hooker tricking my image, and recycled pizza sauce.

It was at this point, lying on my mattress, I started feeling like I was victim to something beyond me. I'd lie there and think, Can I stop this? Can people really forget me, the shop, Leland Harland, Dead Guys, Drowned Girl, all the amateurs? Right now it's money, but can I wake up tomorrow and put an end to it?

So, like I said, I don't fall for notes anymore.

But I rang the doorbell to this one house, and hear a girl crying. It sounds like a little girl, sobbing and inhaling in short breaths, but it's crackling and fuzzy.

"Recorder," I say, readying myself to see some dead people.

I don't fall for notes, but this one had class, an attempt at originality.

The tape recorder, rolling reels under the tiny plastic window, on the floor with wires trailing into the wall. There's no one in the living room, but in the dining room there's four people at the table. Bodies really, their heads filled with holes.

A sprayed trail of red streams out into the living room, a path I squish down to get to this odd contraption hanging over them, this creepy set of strings and pulleys and guns, a stone angel, a smashed clock, a sense something inevitably important is staring at me with a big hole in its head.

A set of strings tied around four guns' triggers leads back over the chairs, and strings itself across the ceiling, then down to a stone angel smashed into a large clock on the table. The clock's glass all fragmented and broken, the hands twisted, the angel lying there on its side.

My eyes slide across the strings and it's easy to figure. Drop the angel, pulley system tugs the strings, strings pull the triggers, heads blow out, clock crunches, time stops.

Time stops.

They stopped it.

I drop the pizza box.

Clicks behind me from the living room, and there's Soto, dark glasses, red curling sinew, pushing in the VCR tape.

People fuzz onto the TV. I guess it's these people, four of them, but actually with faces. They're on the couch I'm sitting on. The camera must have been on the VCR. I look at them, looking at me, and this scruffy fat-faced guy with mischievous eyes speaks a husky, careful voice, and says:

"This all started with Leland Harland's gathering of the greatest artists and minds of our time. After his death, and at his words, 'Leave behind a hideous corpse and a beautiful body of work,' we plan to be remembered after death, to defy death is to take your own life, but listlessly waiting to stop breathing, to feel your heart contract or brain seize up is to truly be at the mercy of, and victim to, something beyond your control, to be at the cruel cold strangling hands of time."

Can I wake up tomorrow and make all this stop?

I watch time count on the VCR, numbers changing, my heart beating and breath running out, immortality pathetically slipping.

No. I can't.

"Holy shit," I say.

"Now you've got it," she says.

She hands me an envelope.

"I never doubted you, Finn." She kisses me on the cheek and walks away, all hips and full of nothing, walks out the door, all hips and gone forever.

I'm left there in this bloody living room with an envelope marked BEAUTIFUL BODY OF WORK.

I open it, and inside is a Pizza Man business card, the red-and-green logo, the small black letters and address of Carson Street. It's thin and meaningless in my hand, but I flip it over, and the back is scrawled DEAR PIZZA MAN—LELAND."

And I sit there for the rest of the day, watching the sun slide down, and the neighborhood outside forget its light into gray dusk shadows, feeling time selfishly tick away, feeling powerless beyond any hope for revival.

Breath.

Beat.

Die.

It was all so simple, so elegant, and that made it the more brutal.

Hours after the sun goes down, on the couch, sitting in the dark, I say, "We're all born to die."

I really would smash some clock somewhere, or put a bullet in a pretentious artist's head to keep this. The shop, the apartment with no carpet, Dave's snoring. It's not much, but it's better then waiting for what's at the end, cause I don't know what's there. And not knowing what's at the end, except that it wants me and will have me regardless of anything I do, disturbs me beyond any hope for revival so much it's disturbing.

"And that pretty much brings us here. All things considered, I can't help but feel a little tricked, a little violated, but anything you believe in is a trick, someone just got you to buy into it. So now you have the whole story of these Reality Show artists, these supposed great minds who could think of nothing better than to kill themselves, to defy Time like it was some kind of strict parent.

"Well, I shouldn't necessarily say that."

I lean back on the wooden chair; its legs scrape the concrete of my apartment.

"I see now that me seeing it this way will most likely be the ascension of Leland Harland to some kind of cult, underground art legend. Soto, you're most likely coming to take pictures, and write REALITY SHOW on my forehead for some sick art gallery I think you're putting together called Reality Show, but, as for Leland, he'll most likely go down as a twisted artist who contrived his beautiful body of work from his peers and direct follows, and stumbling delivery guys.

"It's silly, I know but once you look at time like that, see people dying to avoid it…"

The phone's in my left hand.

"…there's no conceivable going back."

I tap speed dial with my thumb.

"Like battlefield flashbacks—well, what I think they'd be like—I don't think I can ever live normally knowing every clock, every breath, every green light turned red counts my passing to something I know nothing of, and am terrified of. I can see now why people buy into religion, to label where they will go in death, so they can live without fear.

"I don't buy religion."

The phone to my ear, it rings.

"And I don't plan to live in fear."

The revolver's in my left hand, cock back the hammer.

A voice says, "Saigon Express."

"Yeah," I look right in the camera.

Shumon

Theodore Rigby
from *Migrant Workers in South Korea*

Intemperate Thoughts in January

Mercedes Lawry

Monsoon of thought travels the slim electric
circuits, erratic flashes as the whole
tries to make sense of the parts.
Equally driven to hide from the knife points
of winter rain as reasoning fails
to calculate the center of discomfort
and everything collapses in the face of that.

Where are the birds now? Huddling in trees,
damping down their impulses?
A message, generated by a string of words
or the way light is folded into the cavernous clouds,
comes in and takes a space, becomes
another and another as the piano notes turn to wings,
become amazing fish swimming in my blood.

GRAPHITE DRAWINGS BY
ETHAN MURROW

CLOUD COLLECTING WITH THE PINTO BROTHERS documents a group of fictitious siblings determined to ply the stratosphere with questionable aeronautical devices. Huffaker, Lillienthal, Octave, Chanute, Pierpont, and Langley all dream of monumental results and the glow of fame that will follow their grand success in the air. A cacophony of bad judgment never dampens their insatiable thirst for glory.

The Pinto Brothers are part of an ongoing series that deals with obsessed explorers and doomed inventors. All of these characters live dangerously close to disaster, embarrassment, and innovation all at once. Their actions are defined by the catastrophes and accomplishments of their historical peers. The Pintos are very loosely based on the luminary and troubled characters that influenced and interacted with the Wright brothers during their early investigations into flight.

In a variety of desolate locations, using elaborately dysfunctional props and costumes of my own design, I act the protagonist who dreams big yet will probably fall far. As the central figure, I also embroil myself in a history of aspiration filled with brilliant new finds and ignorant mistakes.

Components of this project are collaborative in nature. Vita Weinstein, a photographer and videographer, works closely with me, scouting sites, directing performances, and then shooting still and moving images. Her superb eye and insightful contributions to content and direction help make this project possible.

"LILLIENTHAL'S CURIOUSLY INCORRECT METEOROLOGICAL
PREDICTIONS MADE HIM THE PRIMARY SCAPEGOAT"
GRAPHITE ON PAPER, 60"x144" 2006.

"OCTAVE CHOSE THE LAUNCH SITE ACCORDING TO

"THE BURNING HULK OF JETPACK DIDN'T KEEP
HUFFAKER FROM POSING FOR THE CAMERAS"
GRAPHITE ON PAPER, 54"x36" 2006.

"Octave's maps of the launch site were not to be trusted"
Graphite on paper, 72"x96" 2006.

{ "REVERSING EXTINCTION I, II, III, AND IV"
GRAPHITE ON PAPER, 40"x40" EACH 2005.
FROM EXPLORATION SCIENCE. }

{ "THE HYDROGEN EXPEDITON –
PREPARING TO EMBED THERMO-SENSORS"
GRAPHITE ON PAPER, 18"x44" 2005.
FROM EXPLORATION SCIENCE. }

{ "THE HYDROGEN EXPEDITON –
TEMPERATURE ASSESSMENT" }

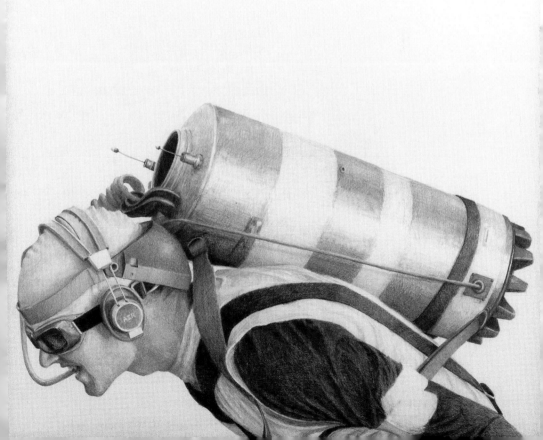

"LAVA COLLECTION —
WELL I DEFINITELY HEARD SOMETHING"
GRAPHITE ON PAPER, 54"x54" 2005.
FROM EXPLORATION SCIENCE.

"DIG A HOLE TO CHINA —
BUCKET Nº 31"
GRAPHITE ON PAPER, 52"x52" 2005.
FROM EXPLORATION SCIENCE.

ETHAN MURROW was born in Greenfield, Massachusetts in 1975 and grew up on a small sheep farm in rural southeastern Vermont. He received his BA in Studio Art from Carleton College in Northfield, Minnesota in 1998, and his MFA from The University of North Carolina at Chapel Hill in 2002. Based in New York, NY he shows his drawing, painting, sculpture and video work both nationally and internationally.

Selected recent solo exhibitions include: Obsolete in Venice, California in November of 2005, Youngblood Gallery in Atlanta in September of 2005, Reeves Contemporary in New York City in June of 2005, and Bucheon Gallery in San Francisco in 2006.

Ethan has received numerous awards and fellowships for his work, which has been reviewed and selected for publication in *The Los Angeles Times*, *Harper's Magazine*, *Art New England*, *Sculpture Magazine,* and *New American Paintings*.

Ethan's work is in many important public and private collections, including The Guggenheim Foundation, Twentieth Century Fox, The Bemis Center for Contemporary Art, and The Burj Dubai.

from Asking for Murdoch

Ray Nolan

It was Foster Murdoch and his father, Charles, and another man Foster
had heard his father talk about for a long time. They were halfway between
Fourth and Third, heading west down Seneca as his father competed for air-
space against the cacophony of Friday afternoon traffic.

"I'm excited by your interest," he said. "Usually you end up in my neck
of the woods because there's no other choice. Scheduling, you know, who's
dropping off Foster and who's picking Foster up. How to make things work
so we can all sit down for dinner together. This is different. I'm really quite
excited."

"Me, too."

They were walking in a line, three across, and Foster was closest to the
street. His father looked the other way and said, "Fos here wanted to see

what I do. And since he's been to the clinic a thousand times, I assumed he must be talking about the bigger picture."

The man's name was Stephan, and Charles pronounced the second syllable with a European accent: Steph-on. Foster had been hoping for something easier, a father-son thing that allowed him to ask the same question three times and not feel stupid. All he really needed was a quick look around so he had at least some idea how to bullshit his way through a thousand words. But somehow Stephan had climbed into the picture, and his involvement unnerved Foster on a purely logistical level.

There was a tiresome quality to the day; the light was mustardy, artificial, and the dampness was almost warm. It was late March, gray and rainy; though the anticipation of spring was real the season itself was faroff. Places like Greenlake and the Arboretum, festive trips come May, were enjoyed only by a sparse contingency of dogwalkers and greenthumbs. The locks were empty of tourists. Downtowners harbored an urgency to beat it home before the early northern darkness.

They made the second light without stopping, working their way toward the water. It seemed to Foster that his father and Stephan shared an implicit understanding that all the real education began there. And yet clearly an agenda hadn't been set forth until now. Stephan listened with quick, democratic nods as his father went over the plan.

"Foster's questions have to do with all the stuff out here," he said, "our work on the ground level. So I thought it might be neat for you to join us and sort of take us through the motions. I thought we might stop first at Clancy's, and you could sort of explain what you did there. Then we could drop by The Rackateer." He put his hand on Stephan's shoulder, took it away, and looked again at Foster. "Stephan's da man, bro!"

"Does mom know we're tied up for a while?" said Foster. "All I told her was I was going downtown to see you."

"Your mom and I talk three times a day—clockwork for the last, what, thirty-some years? Foster here is sixteen years old," Charles said in a nonfiduciary way. "Stephan's got a four year-old and a two year-old. Charming little kids."

Stephan smiled a happily subordinate smile. "The way I see it, the age is charm enough." He pulled at his beard, combing his hands over his cheeks and twisting the hair into a point at his chin. He wore wool socks and Birkenstocks and cargo pants and a white Shetland sweater and John Lennon glasses. His hair needed to be cut. Foster glanced his way, feigning interest as they entered the circus of Pioneer Square.

Businessmen in dark suits were everywhere, sidestepping and shuffling at breakneck speed, trying to escape this place of dreaded burn-outs and alt-rock coffeehouse disciples. This was the population Foster knew here, and for the moment it seemed temporarily overrun. Stephan edged ahead a few steps, steering them to the right along First. Falling behind, Charles stole a moment with his son to catch up.

"So how was school?" he said. "Give me the condensed version. Go ahead and try, Fos."

"No news. It's not like we reinvent the wheel every day."

"You mess up, though. You succeed. That's what I'm saying. Just tell—"

"—All. I know, Dad. I do. That's the thing."

"You had a bad day. I can see it."

"A normal day. I had a normal day."

"You failed your test."

"I didn't have any test."

"That girl," said Charles. "That one girl's not reciprocating."

It was a running joke, ever since he drove Foster and his then eighth-grade girlfriend to see a movie alone. Occasionally after that, Charles had used it as evidence that he would always, no matter what, stay involved in his son's life. To gain his own leverage, Foster had lied that he and Tracy Sternem had lasted a month tops, even though they'd kept hooking up in movie theaters all over Seattle for almost a year.

Two years later the one girl was any girl. Foster could care less; the joke had lost its zip, its panache. Charles let it go so as not to embarrass the poor boy any more.

At the light they crossed First and descended a half-block to Clancy's. It stood on the corner, the cross street small and unkempt enough to impart the bawdy, dubious atmospherics of an alleyway frequently visited by the police. Over the years Foster had surely passed here countless times on family trips to the piers, but he didn't remember ever seeing the bar's mutilated signage. It was now just a mealy piece of yellow wood, the edges rotting. Green and white paint depicting a dancing leprechaun had peeled and faded. The inside was dark and abandoned, and on the door was taped an official notice of some kind protected by plastic laminate.

"So what happened?" said Foster.

Charles nodded at Stephan, and Stephan nodded back.

"Tuberculosis spreads like wildfire in non-ventilated spaces," he said. "Think of being stuck in an elevator for three hours with ten flu patients. So we come in and do the dirty work. It's pretty non-glamorous and potentially menacing. But your dad is a great negotiator. See, it's important for us to believe in the end result. The end result is making people healthy."

Stephan talked fast, and the speed alone was impressive. "Do they get mad?" Foster said. "Do the owners, like, want to kill you?"

Stephan chuckled, then apologized for chuckling.

"Maybe you're more of a businessman. I can see you're coming at this from the other side, which is crucial. It's crucial to be aware of what you're taking away. That's what your dad understands."

Charles spoke up after a deep, highly anticipated breath.

"We don't blame them," he said, "there's no blame whatsoever. It's a potential public health issue because lots of our patients reported coming here. These owners obviously didn't like the sound of it from the first shot fired. Of course, the law would've been null and void if the ventilation in the place looked fine."

Foster's attention wandered to a waify girl smoking a cigarette on the opposite corner. She was looking around suspiciously, though she seemed used to being suspicious. She wore knee-high leather boots, a scrap of red velvet for a skirt, and an orange neon t-shirt that read Fuck You. Don't marry Me! Foster was sure if they waited long enough a Camaro or Trans Am would lure the girl inside if the guy she was waiting for didn't show.

Perhaps because he'd already captained their oldest through the proverbial high seas of adolescence, and because had Angie credited, at least in part, her interest in college academics to certain seeds she'd been able to sow in high school, Charles was glad to see his son momentarily distracted. He liked to think he adhered to the belief that if you press teenagers too hard, it will only impassion their inevitable revolt.

"A little skimpy around the waist, Fos," he said. "A little heavy on the makeup, too."

"Jesus, Dad." But Foster was dialed in again. That was the thing: he had to be dialed in. He turned away from the girl and looked inside the belly of Clancy's, at the stiff wooden chairs overturned on the tables, the empty ashtrays stacked at the bar, the juke box machine with no music playing. "So I take it—what?—you closed them down. It doesn't exactly look like business is booming."

"The system inside is outdated," said Stephan, "and our interviews with patients revealed that a good fifty-percent of them come here two or more times a week. That's more than enough risk. So our investigation turned the potential for public health endangerment into the factual basis for the law to shut them down until the risk has been eliminated."

Maybe there was even more to the way Stephan talked than just speed. Behind the beard, behind the humble slouch and the slight paunch at his belly, the man was painfully exact.

"So you shut them down," said Foster, "and what?"

"Treat the patients," he said. "Make them better."

"But for the time being," said Charles, "Clancy's will remain closed. Maybe I was being too simple earlier. Certain things can be brought up to code. Certain things can be altered and fixed in a snap. But places like this earn a reputation. As you know, Fos, we treat largely the homeless, the sick and the poor. They don't have the wherewithal to change their lives for the better. It's the sad fact. It's the sad fact that they won't follow through with their treatments, and that they'll keep coming back to places like this, and that enough of them together will perpetuate their sicknesses even if the ventilation is brand-spanking new. Ultimately, their sicknesses is our only concern."

The girl had moved on, up toward the Market. They were two blocks off the water, a low fog obscuring the piers, shrouding the boardwalk chowder shops and Space Needle novelty stands and the ferries parked behind them. Foster felt it was his turn again to say something, but he didn't have anything to say.

"So," said Charles, "any more questions?"

"Um, not really."

"Give it time to sink in. The questions will come." He checked his watch and glanced eastward. "The Rackateer, then. Who's game?"

———

They covered most of the ground they would need to get back to the clinic. This time they used Spring Street, working their way slowly back up the hills, and Foster lagged several steps behind. He was confused now about how things worked in the field, and was worried that his confusion would fail him. It had been, when none of it mattered, a simple process, but now the bigger picture frightened him. It had even been simple before his father started talking about reputation. It had been simple minutes ago with Stephan leading the way.

At The Rackateer, one block north of the clinic, they stopped outside for a briefing. Foster knew the place as soon as he saw it. Here was where he and his best friend Darin Blausinghame had scored their first dime bag a year ago, and where they hadn't been back since. It was one of those one-block stretches you went two blocks out of your way to avoid when it was dark. Even now, in the rush hour swarm, the bus stop jammed with people, the threat of some surprise attack made Foster restless.

If there was a sign for The Rackateer, he couldn't find it. All he found was a glass door he couldn't see through, a door of tinted black glass. He looked up at the two stories above him, and found all the windows tinted black.

Stephan scooted close and said, "Things can get a little rough in here. I mean, they have gotten rough in the past. The caseworkers are the real heroes."

"We'll just stay a minute," said Charles. "Basically, Fos, it's your typical big-city shelter. It used to be a dance hall or something, years ago. Hence the name, a mistake in my opinion. The Rackateer doesn't exactly sound too, too tranquil if you ask me." He looked up at the door as though he could see through it. "The patients you see in the clinic? They make it here at one point or another. A lot goes down, bro."

They took the stairs to the second floor, where a plump, worn-looking, thin-haired woman greeted them from a small office separated by a floor-to-ceiling sheet of plexi-glass. She was half-hidden by stacks of papers and smothered in cigarette smoke. The ashtray contained a pile of cigarette butts. A cigarette burned in her pudgy hand.

"Charlie," she said. "'Bout time we saw you here." She looked him over, burying her cigarette in the ashtray. "Denise left about an hour ago with Frankie. They were in here talking about going sober. Apparently Frankie said in one of his clearer moments he wanted her to help him get through the DT's. That woman works hard, Charlie. Whatever you're paying her ain't enough."

"Claude," said Charles, "meet my son Foster. Foster, Claude."

The woman stuck her hand out from the small opening in the plexiglass and shook Foster's hand. "Have a look around," she said. "Just don't touch anything or smile too much. Ain't nothing to be scared about but everything, though I admit it sounds asleep in there. Come to think of it, I betcha Proozer and Wern are sleeping right now. Probably in the kitchen sleeping on the job. Probably dreaming of Costa Rica or something."

"We'll be in and out," said Stephan.

"Do whatever you want. Only you doctors got that right, so enjoy it."

They moved out of the front hall, around the corner to an enormous room with long, buffet-style tables scattered here and there against the far wall. At some of the tables men of various ages played cards, at others men and women both sipped monotonously from matching cream-colored coffee cups. The other wall was lined with low-lying cots, side by side, half of which were occupied by sleeping forms in hooded sweatshirts and oversized pants secured at the waist with strips of flannel, bungee chords, pieces of frayed rope. The black-tinted windows were cross-hatched on the inside with metal bars. White ceramic tile, gleaming underfoot, gave off a meticulous governmental shine.

They stood together where the hallway behind them opened into the main room. Charles scanned the place for any signs that the peace may soon be disturbed. The sleepers, of course, could sleep through anything; poverty had that effect. But the conscious could be violently unpredictable if they sensed an encroachment of any kind. The problem Charles had with the shelters was that they revealed a professional flaw. It wasn't that he felt so bad for specific patients that sometimes on his drive home, the pressure of not allowing himself to feel brought him close to tears. No, that was okay, that was normal given the absurdly uphill battle he faced with most of the people he dealt with. It was, instead, that he wished that some other of the patients—the bad ones, he'd told Kay, the bad people—would just go ahead and die.

But now the quietness of the place, the calm, was suddenly too foreboding. Charles was used to it alone, or together with Stephan or Denise, but it was suddenly wrong to bring Foster here under any circumstances. From the tables heads were slowly turning, and though some of the faces revealed one-time patients, there was no real connection, no established history that made him less of the privileged government doctor who gave them a few meds and ran some critical tests to determine the cause of their racking, incessant cough or systematic fatigue. It was better anyway, even under the most optimal conditions (patients Charles actually knew and who knew Doc), to enter an atmosphere of controlled chaos—people constantly coming and going, arguments over lunch leftovers, whispered plots to steal so and so's welfare check later that day. In these situations the worst of the tension had already built, the buildup had already happened, whereas now the worst was future tense.

And yet Charles had the stupid feeling, at fifty-one years old, that to turn his only son away would be cowardly.

"Come on," he said in a low voice, taking the first steps into the room. "Back there is the kitchen."

As they walked the length of the room Foster was very aware of being stared at, though he felt no hostility toward him. He was very aware that perhaps his age had something to do with this. He felt as though his age entitled him to a measure of decency that otherwise might not exist.

When they reached the back of the room Charles pushed open the door, relieving them of the smell of unwashed bodies, the sour stench of sweat-infused clothes. Though the kitchen was outdated, it was immaculate. Behind the two men—one black, one white, both densely muscled and obviously tall despite their positions at the buffet table—pots and pans hung in neat rows above the sink. There were no encrusted silverware, no congealed plates of food. Spatulas and tongs and basters and enormous wooden spoons were gathered together in a flower vase on the counter; cookbooks had also been arranged there between two microwaves. A pleasant, sugary smell filled the air.

Foster took the men to be Proozer and Wern, and judging from certain bodily evidence he assumed they were more than capable of keeping the place under control. A mosaic of tattoos covered both of the white guy's arms, and a raised scar cut a clean, east-west swath across the right side of the black guy's neck. If they'd been talking, they seemed happy to have the conversation interrupted. Maybe Foster had expected a communal glare his way; he wasn't sure what he'd expected. His father put him at ease with a voice that was clearly comfortable here.

"Gentlemen," he said, "meet my son Foster. Foster, this is Shelton Proozer. Shelton cooks a mean brisket. He also does this barbeque spaghetti thing I haven't tasted anywhere. And then there's Happy Wernell. Word to the wise, Fos: don't call Wern Frank, whatever you do. Call him Hap or Happy or Wern. Wern and Proozer, this is Foster. Foster is sixteen."

Even to Charles his son's age mattered, though it had nothing to do with Proozer and Wern. Though Wern had worked the shelter for years, Proozer had been here long enough to seem as though he'd been here just as long. Together, the two kept the Rackateer lawful enough to stay open and do what little it could do to help.

Wern stood and shook Foster's hand. At full height, facing him, Foster sensed an immediate strategic alliance being formed. He thought at first it was their whiteness, but he also caught Proozer smiling his way. He looked up nervously at his father, who'd struck the famous Charles Murdoch dinner party pose, the hands on hips, come-as-you-are-I-don't-care pose. It was the image everyone kept of him and, to his credit, it was genuine.

"And Proozer," he said finally, lifting one hand from the corresponding hip and gesturing toward the black man. This time it was Foster who reached across the table.

Proozer shook hands amiably. Wern trained a careful eye on his friend and said, "Been a bad day. Prooz's old man passed this morning."

"He went alright," said Proozer. "Mom sez he got up in the night and went to the bathroom. She sez, 'It seemed like such a good sign. I heardz 'em in there singing Amazin' Grace.' He went crazy for that song."

"Who knows what he knew," said Wern. "I say he knew something."

Proozer signaled for Charles to come near. He stood and leaned across the table, meeting him halfway.

"You bring ever'one to the funeral. We'z gonna have a party. I ain't gotta clue when it iz, but ya bring ever'one."

Hearing the news, Charles felt indulged by his own parents' robust health. "I'm sorry, Shelton. Let us know what we can do."

"We're having a quick little wake in an hour or so," Wern winked at Foster. "Goin' down to Pipes soon as Claude let's us loose." He was whispering, encouraging the alliance. Then he spoke up suddenly. "Yo Steven, you come too if ya want. I'd invite the Cap'm, but I figure he's got plenty things to tend to."

So far Stephan had kept quiet, mostly out of respect. He wasn't yet friendly enough with either men to correct his name without sounding like he didn't give a shit about who they were or what they did. When he thanked them on his rounds it sounded hollow and contrived, and when he tried something more loosey-goosey—not saying anything but simply acknowledging them with some haphazard wave of his hand he hoped was more streetworthy—he left feeling as though his nonchalance had discredited them completely.

Now, however, bolstered by Wern's invite to attend an impromptu wake in Proozer's honor, he felt comfortable capitalizing on the invite with unfabricated sincerity.

"I'm sorry about your father," he told Proozer. "You're good to make it in today."

"Yea," said Proozer, "well. I mean, what the hell, 'ya know? Know what I'm sayin', Steve?"

Something beeped in the kitchen. It might've been one of the two microwaves, or one of the two stoves, or maybe an alarm clock stowed away in one of the drawers. The kitchen was wide, and the buffet table that Wern and Proozer guarded contained a multitude of drawers. The beep sounded again seconds later, and Wern procured an oven mitt and a spatula from one of the drawers and made a beeline for the stove.

"Ginger oatmeal cookies," he said over his shoulder. He slipped further to his left, opened one of the wall cabinets, and slid the cookies from the baking sheet onto a plate he'd placed on the counter. Then he brought the cookies over to Foster and said, "Beauty before age, Prooz. Eat up, little Cap'm. As many ya want."

"Stephan's right," said Charles. "You're good to come in, Proozer. It'd be perfectly understandable if you couldn't make it."

"Naw," said Wern, shaking his head. "'Naway. Claude gave me the phone and I demanded he make it. That's how it is, right? Right, Prooz? The ship'll sink without him. Now go ahead and open up those doors, Cap'm. It's getting too quiet in there."

But Charles held his gaze long enough on Proozer to let him know he meant exactly what he'd said. Claude was effective because she was unsympathetic, and it mattered to Charles that Proozer had more sympathy than he needed.

It also mattered, at once when he swung open the door into the main room, that he not linger any more. It was still as calm as before, and Charles knew it was critical to wrap things up before the place filled with drunks looking to stay warm and dry for the night. He recognized, too, as he always did at the shelters, the importance of appearing undaunted by the potential collective force of these masses. Given what the rest of them were up against, it was a dramatic, narcissistic imagining. But his occasional fear of certain risks he took with the job was real.

Turning around, he went straight to Foster and clapped a hand on his son's shoulder. "We should get going," he said. "You're mom—you know your mom, bro." But he immediately felt wrong, with Proozer and Wern around, saying it. Their language—Proozer's imbued with a faintly Southern accent, Wern's narrowly Bostonian—was the real deal, and attempting his own version reduced it to some cheap streetcorner magic act he could conjure on a whim. To compensate Charles returned the favor to Proozer. Motioning him near, he leaned over the table and hugged him very businesslike, very professional, and said, "Tell me when the funeral is. I'll be there no matter what."

"Bring ever'one," said Proozer. "We'z gonna have a party."

Wern said, "Little Cap'm, it's a pleasure. Steven, a pleasure. Doc, don't be a stranger now."

"No, sir."

Only Charles didn't feel himself when they left. He felt as though something big should be bothering him, and this bothered him enough. But not feeling himself was part of the job, and part of the job was ignoring these feelings long enough for them to be replaced by other feelings that weren't part of the job. Back through the main room to the front desk, the ones at the tables stared, and this time Charles didn't think once about where he should or shouldn't have taken Foster. If Foster wanted to see the field, the field was what he needed to see.

———

Down the stairs and out into the street, the Fourth Avenue chaos engulfed them. Four lanes of cars deadlocked and people pushing them out of the way like New York City. The bus forcing its nose into traffic to a symphony of horns played by spent commuters. Up above the clouds were denser and darker and the day's rain that'd been promised seemed close at hand.

They didn't stop to talk, just walked quickly back to the clinic and parted ways in the garage.

"I've heard this and that about the famous Fos," said Stephan. "It was nice to finally meet you." He shook hands with Foster, then turned to Charles. "My stuff's already in the car. See you Monday, Boss." It wasn't his style to wink, but he was uplifted by their trip to the shelter. He would go to the funeral too if the boss agreed it wasn't presumptive but kind.

"I've got to grab some stuff upstairs," said Charles. He was proud of his hire, every day he was proud, but suddenly, with Foster at his side, he felt impregnated with it. "We're right behind you. Say hi to those kids. Catch some zees if you can."

"Will do."

When he was gone, descending the rampway to the lower floors, the silence of the garage imparted a powerful fact of aloneness. Charles knew everyone in the building was gone except maintenance. Before leaving, he'd planned as always to grab his leather satchel containing any necessary home-work for the weekend. But he felt a loyalty to the silence only to leave it behind once, in the Cherokee with Foster. Taking the elevator to the seventh floor and coming back down wasn't an option.

He looked at Foster and caught him looking back. He had a thought that seemed impressive in its cold objectivity: If your teenager takes an interest in something remotely academic, do not think you are responsible. Yet he relished the obvious fact that he was responsible, at least partly. "Let's go," he said, almost zealously, as though leaving this way subjected them to harsh punishment if they were caught.

Foster grinned, shrugging secretly like he was willing to believe in some risk that wasn't there. "Let's do it," he even answered. Like Stephan, he was buoyed by the way their trip had ended. The way it had ended covered his bottom line. As he saw it, he could get five-hundred words from The Rackateer alone, and a thousand easily from the alliance.

———

The rain was more driving mist than anything, and its sleepiness seduced them both. Up over Broadway and back down, a slow crawl into the valley before the mansions and huge, manicured lawns of Madison Park, they were silent. Foster thought about the paper, and wondered if he was even excited to write it. At first this seemed ridiculous, but why did he consider staying in on Friday night and finishing it in one sitting? There was, of course, the issue of Mr. Hambrose, the only teacher Foster cared anything about. Hambrose was tall and thin and feature-strong; he wasn't exactly good-looking, the girls said, but sexy. They raved about his eyes and lips and curly, dust-brown hair— a package they seemed incapable of finding in guys their own age. It didn't hurt that Hambrose dressed down in something other than khakis and bland Polo shirts, occasionally even donning a beat-up-chic St. Louis Cardinals cap from his hometown.

Foster, however, owed his true allegiance to the simple fact that Hambrose could legitimately act like one of the dudes. Earlier in the week, a day after he collected the original paper—an essay requiring each student to chronicle some trip or encounter that made them feel isolated and alone—he met Foster at his desk after the class had ended. "Murdoch," he said, cupping his hand shoulder-high for a buddy slap, "give me the juice." It was all he said and it was enough. Foster slapped his hand and waited for the room to clear out for lunch. Hambrose pulled up a chair and motioned for him to sit down and talk.

"The thing is," he said, "if you didn't excel in here, I wouldn't bother. But that paper was a breeze for you. So go ahead and lay it bare. We'll see if we can't work something out."

Foster was, in fact, so ashamed of his lapse that he'd planned on turning in the paper to Hambrose's box after school to avoid facing the man himself. He'd finally finished it the night before, a record-setting performance in less than an hour.

"You want the truth?" he said, surprised by his candor.

"Don't worry, I can relate."

"I did it on purpose. I mean, it didn't sneak up on me. I've got it right here."

"Forget it," said Hambrose, shooing at Foster like a fly. "You owe me something better. It's the curse of being good at what you do. Of course, I still have to knock off a full grade."

"I just said, 'Forget it for once." Foster felt he had to explain himself until he'd made it clear his failure to perform was nothing personal. "I just wanted to be lazy."

"Be lazy all you want. But not in my class you don't."

Since it was an essay writing course, and since Hambrose's focus of late was on providing the necessary dramatic evidence to support any major claims made in the process, he assigned Foster the task of choosing himself a topic that would substantiate a strong narrative line. All Foster knew was what his teacher's heady talk boiled down to. Hambrose wanted to see and hear and feel things; he wanted scenes and hopefully some dialogue and, if he was really lucky, a few characters that cussed a lot. Making people cuss all the time was Foster's secret weapon, and he figured to use it as long as Hambrose kept leaving red exclamation marks and smiley-faces in the margins.

It didn't take long, that night after being confronted in the classroom, for Foster to decide what to write about. When he was younger, he'd taken trips downtown and watched from the passenger seat as his father gave away Mc-Donald's cheeseburgers to patients he knew by name from the clinic. At six years old it was a powerful thing to witness, and years later the picture of his father playing Jesus had left such a strong impression that Foster questioned if the trips had ever happened. He knew they had, but had they? Unsatisfied with the answer, he'd become prone to making abstractions about his father based on the most superficial evidence. Because he lacked a single sharp suit, or because he shot a ten handicap playing just once a year with his old slice-and-dice Ben Hogan's, Charles Murdoch knew infinitely more than he let on. So he was a wizard in sheep's clothing, a four-sport letterman as modest as Ghandi. Modesty was the word Foster attached to his father most often, though by attaching it he also made him a martyr for the family. There was so much more, Foster was convinced of it, his father could've become than just the city's Director of Public Health.

Foster gave his mother the same props, though her role called for a wider range of talents. All mothers could do ten things at once. They chaired theater committees and planned neighborhood review meetings and stayed abreast of dental appointments all while washing and drying the clothes, making the beds, buying the groceries and fixing the dinners, making plane reservations to visit in-laws in Arkansas, mopping, dusting, and buying new linens to match new comforters ordered online. When Foster considered these achievements, it was no wonder his mother had little energy to enforce the Murdoch Family Rules and Regulations. She really only strictly enforced her kids' obligations at school; since sixth grade Kay Murdoch had noisily warned Foster that a failure to meet every academic deadline would force her to show a certain face she hoped never to show again. She tirelessly replayed the one instance when Angie had slipped in this regard—and even that, she insisted, was a watered-down version of the real thing, seeing as Angie had just simply forgotten. But, she'd instructed Foster, even if Angie had flat-out lied, even if their daughter had very purposely neglected the paper in question (addressing, Kay had proudly recalled, whether or not the murderer in the book The Stranger was actually crazy), the point now was that it would never happen again under her watch.

That was the threat, and so far it had worked. Foster had asked once— when it was okay to ask, when his question wouldn't make him sound like a guilty man desperately trying to eke out some rationale for her irrationality in hopes of sending a message to her subconscious to be easy on him once she learned the truth—he'd asked what about it bothered her so much. Be exact, he'd said. Explain yourself, Mom. There's a reason for everything, you know. Kay had calmly told him he was right, very good point, then said, "It's the least you can do to show up on time and turn in your assignments. Do it and you won't hear a peep out of me."

Driving home, turning off North Pasty Avenue into the ivy-spiked driveway, Foster furthered his conclusion that his loyalty to Hambrose had made

Monday's due date for the essay seem closer than it was. He decided he was also afraid his mother would royally screw him if she found out.

He would stay in tonight and finish the paper if it killed him.

———

Inside the house, warmed by the rosy atmospherics of the kitchen in full throttle, Charles opened up with an effusion of accolades. After Kay Murdoch had done her rounds, kissing husband and son before returning to make the final touches on what appeared to be her specialty, white-sauce chicken lasagna, Charles made clear how he felt about Foster's participation.

"Your son is a compassionate young man with a keen ability to adapt to very diverse and adverse situations. I don't think I'm overstating things, Kay."

"The question is, how does Foster think he did?"

"There wasn't anything to mess up," said Foster, "if that answers your question."

Charles had gone straight to the fridge for one of his famously dark beers, his Belgian imports or Oregon micros. He stood next to Kay as she layered the lasagna, a casual lean against the gas stove. Foster had dropped his backpack on the floor and was busy flipping through the latest Sports Illustrated, a subscription his father still received even though he hadn't followed a single team in any sport since the dismantling of his beloved 1978 Phillies.

"We went to one of the shelters," said Charles, eyeing his wife's work. "I must say, I had my reservations."

Kay looked up at him half-reprovingly. The other half seemed eager to find something in Charles' return gaze that told her she was wrong to be concerned.

"Honey," he said, "the lasagna looks amazing."

Kay took a stem of fresh rosemary from the herb vase and threaded the spine. "Did you have fun?" she called out, looking over her shoulder at Foster. When he didn't answer she turned and faced him. The difference between Angie and her little Fos, manifest in his perfectly normal unresponsiveness, gave her tension headaches nonetheless.

"Lasagna!" she boomed. "Did you see we're having lasagna, Fos? I even doubled the batch!"

"Hey dad," said Foster, "did you ever see that Hagler/Hearns fight?" A piece on some super lightweight Vietnamese boxer had returned him to the video Darin kept of the three-round slugfest between the famous 70's era middleweights. Though uncoordinated, Darin's brilliant analytical mind and holy passion for sports had combined to create a wizkid historian on everything from Seattle Slew to Franz Beckenbauer to George Gervin. By the time he entered high school, his copious knowledge of mythic rivalries had elevated his dopey-eyed coolness to an art form no one his age could touch. In the process his ineptitude as an athlete had been dropped from the rib-poking banter that hounded him his middle school years. His friends, Foster primarily, seemed won over by the idea that it was far better to be king at some relation to the sporting world than to be mediocre at the sports themselves.

"Weren't there a couple fights?" said Charles. "Wasn't it one of those Ali-Foreman things? Or was it Ali-Spinks? If my memory serves me correct—"

"Three rounds," said Foster. "You'd know it if you'd seen it. I'll get the tape from Darin."

Kay fed the stove the casserole, shut it crisply and poured a glass of Merlot from the decanter on the counter. She suspected, by the simple fact that he hadn't yet mounted the stairs and returned wearing something more Friday night hip, that Foster was staying in. She watched him at the long oak table she'd gotten years ago when they first moved to the house. She'd been thinking lately that her 1982 renovation of the kitchen, complete with imported Spanish tile, eight-burner gas Merro with side griddle, glass fridge and Tuscan-inspired fireplace, lacked a certain something that couldn't be replaced. The rest of the house was replete with splashy Chihuly bowls and the verdantly folkish Clementine Hunter originals Charles' parents gave them every Christmas.

But Kay's decorating was busy to begin with. Instinct had led her to cram the corners of her five bedrooms with night-stand tables upon which family pictures reigned supreme: pale, freckled, eight-year old Angie in Baha, her skin a dangerous crimson, standing proudly aside the 133-pound Marlin caught with the help of a drunk Mexican who lectured in his native tongue despite the fact that one else on the charter spoke more than the obligatory Spanish howdy-do's; Foster in Little League, before his precious Dutch Boy blonde turned short and brown, before he gazed into Niemann-Marcus windows to check his acne, before his seventh-grade Izods succumbed to the latest Abercrombie & Fitch hybrid of grunge rock and prep school; Charles in his pre-med school sixties, his sleepless, twenty-four hour hospital shift seventies, his long-awaited eighties, his searching, relief-effort nineties, his last, restless (Kay's word) first year of the new century; and Kay herself, her striking olive skin reddening pleasantly over the years, her hair shorter and shorter until the kink in it morphed into an idyllic bronze bob tamed with flecks of gray. She understood she had gone well into older age, had slimmed when no slimming was needed, widening only at the hips and in a muscular way she was happy to show off. But her dilemma with the house she kept silent, for fear of arousing Charles' interest in downsizing before their time. More and more she panicked that the house would collapse without either of her kids to pick up after, and more and more she worried over ways to preempt it. She thought perhaps she'd grounded herself too squarely in her trademark aesthetic of more is more, and wondered if it was finally better to put function over form, to purge the house of its museum clutter and go minimal. But being modern was different than becoming modern, and at her age it seemed desperate, the kind of thing Hallie Tellip might do without her Prozac to make her unflagging and austere.

Still, a worried mind was a worried mind, and it happened more than it should. At dinner Kay posed the kitchen question spontaneously, as though she wasn't at all concerned but merely interested, and as though her interest was whimsical in nature.

"The kitchen," she said. "What do you men think about the kitchen? I'm just looking around and I wonder if it needs something. A little more light, maybe."

Charles said, "It's yellow. How much lighter can you get?"

"Plenty." Kay was strong on the subject, and glad to divert the initial question at least a little. "There are all kinds of shades, and a million other colors. It's just a thought. I just thought of it now."

"I've never noticed the yellow," said Foster. "That's probably a good thing."

An accomplished chewing sound filled the silence long enough for Kay to strategize a deeper probing on the subject. The trick was to sound circumspect about the whole thing, though clearly interested, as she was, in the opinions of her two men.

"I mean, I was kind of wondering about pink. Pink with maybe some flowers painted here and there." She decided instead to shock them from their listlessness by going in hard, and watched with girlish anticipation as their leery faces turned on her. "Top of the line custom work, Charlie. Nadine Brockmeyer went with this flashy new contractor from Kirkland. Apparently he used to be some IT guru, some back-end database guy. Apparently he does these great murals. Nadine said he's an artist who's finally getting to do his life's work."

"I would not," said Charles, "put flowers in the kitchen." He tempered this by placing a hand on her shoulder. "If you want a different color, we'll do a different color. But no roses, no flowers period. That's my one request."

"I'm with Dad," said Foster. "Then we'd have to get two Jack Russell Terriers and name them Cotton and Bunny."

"What if I just spruced things up a bit?" said Kay. "Some recessed lights, maybe."

Charles started eating again so she wouldn't suspect him of wondering what had gotten into her. The very thought of the kitchen, her beloved kitchen, getting a makeover after twenty some-odd years gave Charles the sudden feeling that his wife was hiding some bigger piece of information she knew he would condemn outright.

"We could do new lights," he said. "Sure." To discourage further conversation about the issue, he asked Foster his plans for the evening. "I can't remember when you stayed for dinner on a Friday night."

"The paper," said Foster through a mouthful of lasagna. "I figure I may as well finish it while it's fresh. It's dead tonight, anyway."

"You know, your old man's done a few papers in his day. And your mom was a Religion major."

"Religion and history," said Kay. "The two go hand in hand, really."

A loud pop came from the fireplace, where three mature oak logs burned. It was tradition every Friday night, so long as the season supported it. Charles came from a family whose cloying formality disappeared at the feet of natural disaster. He'd watched his father curse crazily during their escape of Hurricane Camille, and had delighted in the fierce outward emotion his mother showed when herding them into the basement as tornados shredded whole Magnolia trees and tore sagging, Depression-era farmhouses from their foundations. The reason, then, his sister and brother had taken the task of their winter firebuilding to heart wasn't for its coziness but for the chaos it represented in the wild. Only when the kids' lives were at stake did their parents manage to fall apart, and only then did they seem most human.

Now, however, the fire was just catharsis after another week lived. There was nothing to look forward to in natural disasters, especially not the kinds that threatened the city. Forget boiling seas and riptide flooding and those Natural Geographic winds that made streets look like they'd been put together in miniature, whole scenes synthetically reproduced to make the unreal real: clay lightposts bent to breaking points, plastic cars glued to the sides of cardboard buildings, wheeling trashcans suspended mid-air by fishing lines tied overhead to an out-of-view ceiling. No, here the talk was all earthquakes and volcanoes, a different mantle of mayhem entirely. As far as Charles could tell the city wanted one or the other. They were desperate for it, the local papers consumed by its local fault lines, the clashing of fault lines and the disastrous force of their clashing, and of its beatific Cascade range whose dirty little secret foretold a much greater destruction than that caused by the native patron saint of destruction, Mt. Saint Helens. Charles was so unenamored by the hype that he no longer feared the reality of it. He stayed clear of the neighborhood earthquake preparedness meeting Kay had put together at Peggie Leure's house, and when she prodded him to join the collective effort he asked why everyone was so excited to prepare for something that, according to the genius analysts on the six o-clock news, would more or less vaporize them anyway? "This isn't nuclear war," Kay had responded, but Charles wouldn't hear of it. He said he'd done the whole natural disaster routine already. He said Kay had done it, too, and was foolish to welcome any of it back into their lives.

That was in January, and it was the first time Charles had realized his wife was right in her diagnosis of him at the start of the year: he was restless, and it was because he was getting older. Charles neither agreed or disagreed. He said she wasn't giving him enough credit. But he also said, "These things come and go, they pass, Kay," which, as he saw it, was a tidy way of acknowledging they both were right to a point.

Since then there'd been a tempering of his outward person and of the mind his wife couldn't read, no matter how well she knew him. He stopped revising their living will, he stopped the jogging he'd recently resumed after the years of constant pounding had reduced his knees to raw cartiledge. He submitted he was restless, but was sure he didn't exactly fear getting older. Eventually he was able to communicate this to Kay, who seemed in the last month literally aroused by the possibility of spending more time at their house on San Juan and finally doing the whole African safari thing they'd talked about for years. Charles couldn't remember the last time they'd had such a string of momentous sex. He couldn't remember the last time they'd had so much sex period. The last month Kay had performed in bed like a whore, and he mounted her as though she was someone else's wife, their sex a secret thing done three nights a week before he went back into hiding. At work he found himself distracted by images of her begging him to get her off one more time, and by images of himself acting like some kind of vigilante, saying things he'd never said, repeating them over and over because every time he said them Kay did this thing with her eyes that made her look like she was having a seizure. Over the years she'd strictly forbidden him to enter her other hole, a fantasy Charles had repeatedly urged on her in the throes of lesser passion, though when he asked several weeks ago she directed him to the bedside table, to the drawer where he kept his keys and wallet and his old parking tickets he'd never gotten around to paying. "Vasoline," she gasped, "you'll have to lube up." Even so it was a tight fit, but Charles was so consumed by the actualization of his fantasy that he'd barely made it inside before he exploded with a murderous scream, buckling in half on top of her, still lodged in the place Kay had been unable to consider, just two months prior, a viable option for her husband's sexual fulfillment. That she'd had the Vasoline at the ready only encouraged the feeling Charles had that his wife's horniness, while surely temporary, was not at all spontaneous. Granted she'd proved this point already; numerous times she'd called the office early in the day to tell him specifically what she had in store later that night. But Charles figured you never knew, even if you knew. Maybe, as he bragged to himself about this prowess Kay showed for which he couldn't help but take at least partial credit, she was debating when to confess it was the Viagra speaking, a quick, secret solution to a problem that embarrassed her and, she thought, would embarrass Charles as well. Of course, in this case Charles figured the opposite. He figured he wouldn't care what the Viagra said about him that his wife had to seek the miracles of modern science to awake the beast within. But in truth he didn't know if he would care or not, that was the thing. You just never knew.

Porch

Sandra Simonds

It's not that I need your drum roll chest to slip
into the saxophone's long brass throat
or that this riverwater folds and folds like turmoil's
patchwork quilt
or that I roll over
in my sleep like an insomniac in need of warm milk
but today a little boy poked
the eye out of a sparrow
and it looked
like a raisin
on the cement

———

day that divides / the black arithmetic
of the bird and bad weather that
carves out its flight path—
(the husky voices of live oaks, the roach
that crosses the kitchen tiles
to the blob of boysenberry jam) &
I can take

———

what I want and leave
the rest   or step through that doorstep

into homelessness's long hall of family portraits
    that wince, grin, giggle
       and tick-tock like clocks and toys

———

you were so proud of my voice
    and knew the words so well
  that you would hum the tune
      whenever the tune
hummed back to you
     like the sharp wing underneath the air
that splits form
  into its whistle and bones

———

despair sounds similar
but so does splendor and what
    does it mean to be the whistle
 of some gorgeous day
    that counts and calls
out to its greenish plants and waters?

———

situated inside the broken hand
   that is a mirror in its last attempt to grab the reflection
of that mirror's light—
    the dog stayed quiet inside
   his dream of squirrels—

        and if a scream   punctuated the neighbor's sleep
      like the disappearing trail
   behind the dusk
     what would it matter to that gorgeous day
  gone into its yellow-
        grass geography?

—

   to reconstruct the sparrow from one black feather
to the next, from the speckled egg's sour yolk
to the boy's swiss army knife
        against a world of forking veins
  would be a misconception
    because the clarinets won't yield
 their jazz secrets
     and neither will
this house of broken birds

from You Were Born Inside

Jacob I. Evans

Draped from the window under a chattering clock cans of sometime on the shelves the day when my brother was born the wall in the backyard fell over the front steps had delicate mosaics between the bricks beach glass pebbles from the front of the world collected in his apron squeezing the milky full backs of jacaranda blossoms gathered in a circle in the shade the insects and relatives stroked his skullcap and held his sleeping fingers in a pot of ink to signal something an indelible plastic in their perfume a shifting of letters grows out of the backs of kitchen chatter the July heat didn't bother anyone

An empty coffee can split open your lip and when you fell from the top almost severing your tongue with your teeth it was held together by string we built torture chambers out of Lincoln Logs when you told me over four hundred miles of phone line about doing acid under the tree at school which evaporated in your sketchbook into faces the house wanted to swallow you up maybe it did when they put the knife to you you made the most horrible noise I had ever heard or will ever televised tumors broken bedroom door flaps in the breeze carving up the idea of you a banjo with its back open tries to get back over miles of highway

Icon of loyal bird tornado reeking breath everywhere the mouth touched is staircase the color of a deep Brahmin dengue reeking palms of criminal ideation on the windowsill growing into there is a doorbell on the other side of the house no one uses it the door creeks a dent around the room another fist through drywall piles of watercolor on newsprint stuffed into a high shelf it will come alive when we dig up all of the bones from under the tree and hang them in a mobile that goes round on twine above the birthing bed replace with a placenta wrapped in a towel so the tree will grow up strong

Statues

Matthew Modica

I've been at this place many times before, but never like this, my cloudbreath dissolving into pale sky, you beneath the mute earth rather than beside me, hands in your pockets and eyes fixed on the statue above your brother's grave. No, never like this, murmuring faces trapped behind ashen veils, and shrieking crows in skeletal trees, and me no longer afraid. I was quiet then, always quiet, too afraid to say anything, and even at the very end, as you lay in bed, your eyes darkening, I remained as you taught, and though I wanted to tell you, I saw you were afraid, and I wanted you to be so, I wanted that power over you, and then you were gone.

So it was that blustery morning the spring Ma left and you didn't know what to do, so we went to the lake, we climbed into your rusty brown pickup with the ripped vinyl seats spewing yellow sponge cake stuffing and the vents that whistled cold air and went fishing. On the shore I cast the lure against the sky, listen I cast it the way you taught, wrist relaxed but snapping, feel the line escape from the spool, follow it chase the lure through the sky, I did all that, I watched it arc through the sky, I saw the sun burning through the clouds, but the line snagged on a dead branch emerging like a serpent from the water, and you shouted damn it, god damn it, go out and fix it. A family came walking along the shoreline, and your voice lowered as you watched them walk, the two boys and the girl, the mother and the father, the dog, and you watched as the boys poked and pushed each other until the broad-chested father dropped his wife's hand and picked them up on either arm, draping a laughing son over each of his wide shoulders. I said, but it's too far out, it's only a silver spinner, why can't – you turned and smacked my head like always, it was for my own good, I needed to learn to do things right, nobody made it anywhere in life screwing around, your brother spent his life screwing around, if he hadn't been such a jackass – take the rowboat, that goddamned rowboat over there – you didn't care if it was broken down, I was going to fix the goddamn line.

Remember how I climbed into that old rowboat, how it creaked and shook as I swung my legs unsteadily over the prow, how the soft hull wood splintered between my nervous fingers, and how you stood there, arms fold-ed, eyes squinted against the sun which had burned away the clouds, and behind you the family down the shoreline watching as they might a parade in town, the woman's arms around the girl's shoulders, the boys' small fingers tugging at their father's pant legs, and you said what are you waiting for, and I knew then what I was going to do. I picked up the broken paddle and shoved off, the wind and water whispering their instructions, and I listened to the wind and the water, you taught me to listen, if that's one thing I learned it was to shut up and listen and so I did, I listened to the wind and water and what they told me to do, the rest of the world was silent and still, nothing moved except the boat and the woman's swirling auburn hair, you stood like the statue in the cemetery, the sun shattered on the water, and when I passed the dead serpent branch I looked back to shore, my heart in my throat, sun spots in my eyes, the family standing like storefront window mannequins, the wind and water crying and wailing, and I grabbed the side of the boat, shifted my weight, rocked high, higher, the world turning, the sun eclipsed, and then I was in the green water.

The water was cold and laughing it punched me in the stomach my breath gone my shoes my jeans my jacket pulling me down my hands useless the wind blowing frozen, I heard shouting from the shoreline it was the family they were running toward you but you stood like the statue then you all blurred everything refracted the water pouring in my mouth kept coming I couldn't swallow my lungs burned my heart burned my chest an inferno. I submerged for a moment it was a black and filthy silence the hope crept in maybe I was wrong please let me be wrong it was so tiring my clothes like a coffin and then back into the morning air my needled breaths painful lake filling my mouth I could not shout I could see the shoreline you were standing there the dog was barking the wind icy I was so tired and I wanted to be wrong but I wanted to give up it was too hard

sinking down down on my back the water was green my eyes were open the sky through the top of the lake like through the other side of a mirror the sun a pat of butter melting on a green table the bottom of the lake a million voices clamoring their distant calls echoing their hands pulling at the cuffs of my jacket the waist of my jeans the laces of my shoes their fingertips caressing my cheek brushing my neck tugging at my hair I grew lighter lighter weightless the sun was melting the water was warm I was floating down breathing in and out in and out breathing the water. I did not meet any dead ancestors like in the books you get from the TV not my grandfather who fell and hit his head that night remember the night you shoved me into the closet because I reminded you not your brother who I never met your brother who spent his life screwing around your brother who you were supposed to be watching no silhouettes standing in a field of white light reaching out to me welcoming me loving me forgiving me for what I reminded you of my life did not flash before my eyes nothing not the way your teeth glinted in the dark not the way your eyes burned hollow not the way the red leaves fell around the statue that day only the sun melting into a shimmering yellow cloud and the milky green water and the embracing hands below me I was weightless and free and free and happy and I wasn't afraid and I didn't care if you were angry and I was relieved yes relieved there would be no more screwing around nobody would be smacking my head nobody would have to look at me anymore nobody would be reminded no more brothers no more statues nothing nothing but calm quiet the noise in my head gone the hands caressing me the sun disappearing into night everything peaceful

then a noose around my neck choking me strangling but it wasn't your arm I knew it wasn't and I was ripped from my sweet dream and onto the shore the lures silver glinting in the sun the reflected light a pinwheel by your feet you whispering oh christ oh and the man shouting call an ambulance his breath hot on my neck the sand cutting my skin the water fluming up my throat my chest heaving ribs cracking heart breaking. The man said what were you doing what were you thinking and you, you, what were you doing what were you thinking how could you just stand I don't understand how you could just, and you were silent, the one time I wanted to hear your voice, to tell me I was wrong, and you were silent, and though my eyes were closed, I knew your eyes were helpless, helpless like always. I opened my eyes and I could see your boots, your calves, and my fishing pole on the ground where I left it, and I thought about how you always told me to learn from my mistakes, but you never realized I wanted you to teach me, to pick me up and throw me over your shoulder, to rub my head, not smack it, and then I saw it was because you were ashamed so you hid behind helpless eyes.

———

Years later, as you lay on a thin mattress, I sat beside you in silence. Through the half-parted curtains next to your bed a lawn lay in a violet-streaked afternoon, and beyond a hedge row marking the grounds, a stand of willows bent toward a glassy pond, and I did not look at you. You shifted, I turned my gaze to your frightened eyes, as hollow and helpless as I remembered, and as you struggled to prop yourself with a feeble arm, your pale face plunging into the light falling through the glass, through hoarse breaths you asked me what it was like. Death, you said, though I knew what you were talking about, I knew exactly what you were talking about, and I watched you struggle, I saw how frail you were, your emaciated limbs, your withered face, the hollows of your cheeks. I saw your frailty, and I saw your pleading and terrified eyes, and I said nothing. I was silent, and you fell back from exhaustion, your thin arm unable to support the weight, and your head turned, you looked at me, past me, and I watched your eyes as they grew dark and darker still.

———

Now, on this winter afternoon, I watch the last of the visitors shuffle out, their feet crunching frozen snow beneath leafless trees. Through the black branches I see the statue where you used to stand in silence, tufts of snow on its wing tips, helpless to shake itself of the cold, and I wonder what it was like for you.

Body Craft: Frankenstein

J.R. Toriseva

1.

There are no guarantees; still, I attended five of the four classes
designed to help me stay in my body, to remain present.
You see, I'd been stopping in, only once or twice every day or so
to check on my heart, to brush these mossy teeth.

2.

Mostly I was living in my other body
the one in South Africa
that body was having a lot of problems.
Couldn't keep off the damn linoleum floor.
Major things.
I had to stay with her September, October and November before
she'd stop shaking.

I built these tongues, hearts, mother-in-laws, immune systems
to run on their own
but that's not the way it always turns inside out.

3.

Above McClure's beach
in a rush of glory mat
in a flurry of sedge nettle
pushing through the rocky slope

ignoring the dainty curling tendrils
of the common vetch
she stood, belly arcing
with child and flew through.

It was my mother
falling back into me.
Our spines passed
then were parallel once more

Two ammonites
settling into air, then sand
All amniotic fluid bled
Curves matched.

Only the katydids heard,
turning their slender necks
before continuing on to granite,
before twisting their ankles on rice.

As Luck Would Have It

Claudia Burbank

One morning, early, down the sleeping street,
a river, unstoppable as a lover rushing in,
swept her off the bed, feet-first, out the door
past the pyramids of a fruitstand (those years
she'd have died for a single bite of orange)
and windows of supple loafers, peau de soie pumps
posed as if to break into a fox-trot,
sped her like a log around the corner where
spectacles in tidy rows watched from a shop,
spectacles like those in the death-camp heaps as
racing by the cinema, the latest
golden girl kissed a golden boy but
already she had skimmed ahead, picking up speed
past the jeweler's velvet necks, velvet fingers,
stripped by the close each day when her hem
for a second caught the French cleaners awning,
suits and dresses hung like recent skins
the living crawled from, then plunging
by showrooms, plumped, pillowed, table-set,
folded *Times* as if people lived there,
good, decent people like you, like me, as she sluiced
by the 6:10, city-bound commuters still
dozing, oblivious, tracks covered over when
purling, swirling, torrents raised her over
shade-drawn windows, disappearing stories, receding
trees like little islands and the white gasp of spires till
everything was water, water and her
and brilliant and unanswered.

Welcome Wagon

Joanne Lowery

I'm so pleased you've chosen our modest town
and my humble backyard on which to land
your impressive craft, and yes, I see
you have locked the lever to stop its spinning.
You mean to stay. I have a futon

in the basement where you can rest your lime limbs.
No need to worry about fluorescence rubbing off
on the sheets, no need. No, I didn't know
you were allergic to strawberries, but I can offer

a California peach and a sheaf of pamphlets
about our community, this one showcasing our schools.
Anything you don't understand, just ask.
I'm my own realtor and can show you

a navel, a condominium of memories,
the uterus I just know you're going to love.

The Made-for-TV Movie of My Life

Miriam Parker

It all broke at once, the story of me, my baby, and my teacher, Joe Rogers. A
local reporter, the father of one of my classmates, heard that I was pregnant.
And I guess the baby got all messed up because of this medicine, Accutane,
I was taking. Somehow, that reporter dude got ahold of my sonogram, too,
and after his initial report on the eleven o'clock Eyewitness News, all of
them descended. CNN, FOX, Channel 4, they were all there with their trucks
and their satellite uplinks, outside my school, outside my house, outside Joe
Rogers' building in Jersey City, hounding us all as we came and went. *People*
magazine named me "Lolita of the Year." Matt Drudge had a new headline
about me every day from "Suburban Slut" to "Alien Baby Mama." I read it all.
Every story about how a stupid teenager on a dangerous medicine had slept
with her teacher and then had a baby with three hands and one lung.

Finally, after Joe Rogers went to jail, everyone went away. I moved into my own apartment and got a job at the zoo. I thought I would have some peace. Then, Sara Ann Schwartz called.

"Jill," she said. "This is Sara Ann Schwartz." She paused as if I would know who that was. I didn't.

"Hi?" I paused the DVD I was watching: "Best of the 80's Game Shows."

"You may have seen my films, *Castle of Woe* and *You Don't Live Here Anymore*. Or my play at the Public Theater, *Astroblonde*?"

"Sorry, I only watch game shows. Would you, perhaps, have been on *Wheel of Fortune*?" I was sick of fake entertainment people bugging me. I just wanted to watch *Press Your Luck*.

"No." The sweet tone was gone now.

"Then why are you calling me?"

"Jill. I'd like to meet you," she said.

"No."

"Please?"

"Why? Because I've been on more TV stations than you have? Or maybe because I fucked my teacher and you only wish you had?"

"No, because…because I'm going to play you in the docudrama."

"The NBC one or the ABC one?"

"CBS, actually."

I didn't know about that one. "I wish they had gotten Natalie Portman."

"You don't look anything like Natalie Portman."

"Or at least Tara Reid." I flattened out one of the cardboard boxes by stepping into the middle of it. It made a great popping sound, so I flattened two more.

She paused. "Listen, I would like to meet you. For coffee. Or dessert. My treat. I'll come to you. Jill, I know you're not doing anything now. Besides, I'm across the street. Just give me thirty minutes."

I looked around. I had unpacked my collection of headless dolls arranged in size order on the shelf above the TV, my vintage posters of Coney Island freaks and my calligraphy set. But it was quiet without anyone else there, even with the TV on. I had never lived alone before and I was bored. So I went. I let Sara Ann Schwartz buy me ice cream at the Baskin Robbins downstairs. She asked me questions about my childhood and my family and how this situation has changed it all.

As I told her about how I always wished I had a little sister, I thought about the last time I saw Joe Rogers. It was at the court house, on the day that the verdict was read. He was wearing a suit that didn't really fit him, way different than the logo T-shirts and corduroys he always wore to school. And his goatee was shaved. His face was so clean and his eyes looked so sad. For a minute, that day, I felt awful. Like it was my fault that his life was ruined. I thought maybe I shouldn't have let him kiss me in his classroom after school that first time. But then I looked at the reporters surrounding me and my lawyer pushing us forward so that I couldn't even say that I was sorry to him and I realized that my life was ruined too. I would always be that girl from the news.

When I almost started crying, Sara Ann Schwartz stopped talking and petted my hand. It felt nice, so I let her keep doing it. I think she thought we were really connecting. But maybe she tricked me a little because when she asked if she could observe me for a few days, for some reason I said yes.

———

Now, Sara Ann Schwartz has been living in my Hoboken apartment with me for three weeks. Sometimes she just "observes" me as I work on my calligraphy project: "History's Biggest Motherfuckers." I've organized them in alphabetical order. I started with writing just "Adam" on a pink index card. I wrote "Hitler" on the bottom of my shoe and walked around on it until it was totally rubbed off. Now, I'm up to "Roman Polanski", which I've written in silver pen on the side of a cast iron cauldron I got at a garage sale. I'm very good at calligraphy. I needed to do something while all the reporters were camped outside my house, and I was eight months pregnant. So I took a correspondence course. I got an A.

That's actually how Joe Rogers and I got together. He told me that he liked my handwriting and I helped him make the bulletin boards in the back of his classroom. Every day after school for about two weeks, I came to his classroom and we cut out letters. Then, on the day that we were supposed to finish, when I got to his classroom, it had a shade on the window. Instead of finishing the display (the only words left were "adverb" and "personal pronoun"), we had screwed on the windowsill. Then we screwed every day after that for six months. I guess, looking back, it was kind of dumb. I mean, it wasn't even that fun.

———

Sometimes, Sara Ann asks me questions. Last week, she followed me to work every day, and sat behind me as I did my job, taking tickets at the Bronx Zoo. During my lunch hour, she followed me on my daily tour of the Children's Zoo.

"Why do you always go to the Children's Zoo?" she asked as we walked through the twisty path.

"I like to pet the prairie dogs," I said. They're soft and small enough to hold comfortably in my hands. My friend Pee Wee, the Children's Zoo Plains Expert (we call him the "Animals Smaller Than Both Fists Expert"), lets me hold them for as long as I want.

"Do you think you are mourning your lost child?" she asked.

"No," I said.

Later in the week, the Arachnid House manager, Alejandro, told me that he had seen Sara Ann in the Children's Zoo, petting the prairie dogs all afternoon and singing, "Rock-a-bye baby" really softly.

I was taken aback. "How does she know that I like to do that?" I asked. "I haven't done it all week. Did YOU tell her?"

"No!" he said. "Your actions in the Children's Zoo are entirely confidential with me." He closed his locker with more force than usual. The noise made him jump.

"Who did, then?"

"I don't know," he said.

"Well, SOMEBODY told her!" I said, cracking my knuckles.

He was cowering now, the people who work at the zoo are all a little bit fragile. "It was Pee-Wee," he said. "She took him out for drinks after lunch on Tuesday and he caved after a coconut margarita."

"NOBODY WAS SUPPOSED TO TALK TO HER!" I yelled.

"Don't yell at me," he said, and scurried out of the room.

Sara Ann studied method acting at NYU and says she has to observe me in my natural habitat. She says she will cut her waist-length hair short and dye it red for this part so she will look like me. She will gain ten pounds for the role, although I weigh at least thirty pounds more than Sara Ann. She tells me that on camera, the ten pounds will look like thirty. I'm not sure I buy this whole "method acting" bullshit. I think it's just an excuse to waste time. But to be honest, I didn't really sleep well in my apartment before Sara Ann started sleeping on the couch. It makes me feel better to know she is there. Even if she does snore.

———

Today, we are going back to my hometown, Stirling, New Jersey, so she can see where the "real scenes" of *Three Hands in the Cradle: The Jill Baker Story* took place. I've stopped reminding her that *Three Hands in the Cradle* is based on my actual life, and it is not just some abstract concept. She can't seem to wrap her mind around it. On the train, we discuss the fact that I have been dating women lately. She wonders if it is a reaction to my relationship with Joe Rogers, if I feel that he betrayed me and that I am now afraid of penises.

"This is why I'm not in therapy," I say. "I'm not afraid of penises, I'm just attracted to women. I've always been attracted to women."

"Maybe you should be," she says.

"I am!" I say.

"No, in therapy, I mean."

"Don't give me any of that Hollywood bullshit," I say. She writes that down.

"Why aren't you dating anyone now?"

"It's hard to find someone to love," I say.

"Are you afraid of commitment?" she asks.

"I date women," I say. "You can't be afraid of commitment with women."

She nods, as if she knows. I realize that I know nothing about Sara Ann Schwartz's life.

"Are you dating anyone?" I ask.

She is silent.

"Where is your apartment?" I ask.

Silence.

I notice that she is wearing my pink and gray argyle socks. I have not lent these socks to her, which means that she has stolen them out of my dresser.

"Bitch," I whisper.

"What did you say?"

"I called you a bitch."

"Why?"

I point at her feet.

"Because I have cleaner sneakers than you do?"

"No, because they're my socks, bitch."

She blushes. "Oh, sorry."

"They're my favorites." I poke her in the shoulder. Hard. She winces.

"I just want to feel more like you, Jill."

I cross my arms in front of my chest.

―――――

My mother picks us up at the train station in her 1987 Oldsmobile Cutlass Supreme.

"Is this the car in which you were impregnated?" Sara Ann asks as we walk toward the car that has a few rust spots on the passenger side as a result of an experiment I did with some vinegar and an ice pick. It didn't work.

"No," I say. "We never did it in a car. Besides, don't talk about that in front of my mother."

She makes a note on her pad.

"Hello, Mrs. Baker," Sara Ann says as she gets in the back of the car, scooting to the middle, away from the melted crayon on the passenger side seat. "It's an honor to meet you."

"The pleasure is mine," my mother says.

"Please. You're too kind. For the duration of this trip, please call me Jill," Sara Ann says. "And I'll call you Mom."

"Why?" My mother turns on the car.

"I want to inhabit Jill."

"If you say so," my mother says. "It's not a great place to be, I can tell you that much." She does not look in her rearview mirror as she reverses and almost hits a truck. I scream. She hits the brakes.

"Mother!" I say.

"Mother!" Sara Ann says.

"Well-done," my mother says. "You've really got my Jill."

"This is creepy," I say.

"This is..."

"Shut up."

"Shut up."

"I mean it."

"You girls! Stop bickering," she says as she drums along to "Paradise City" on the steering wheel. She honks the horn at the end of the song and then continues, "It's as if you had a sister, Jill."

"But worse."

"But worse."

Then, I lean through the seats and punch Sara Ann Schwartz. Her nose starts to bleed and my mother pulls over. She sees this much in the rearview mirror. I adjust it so it is pointed at the street and not at the back seat. Sara Ann says that she is fine, that this is part of the process, the anger part. We should pretend that she is not there.

We do.

When we get to Old Stirling Road, Sara Ann is taking notes with one hand and holding a tissue under her nose with the other. I can feel her observing the houses, the Ford Tauruses and Hyundais in the driveways, the plastic ornaments on the lawns. Our lawn has a plastic bee with wings that spin in the wind. When I was little, we had a family of gnomes: a mommy gnome, a daddy gnome, and a little girl gnome. When the story about me and Joe Rogers hit the news, someone left a two-headed baby gnome made out of Play-Doh on the lawn. I thought it was in bad taste. This is not in the movie. In the movie, we will have a flamingo.

My mother is asking me about my job at the zoo. I've always loved animals. And ripping paper. It is a perfect job for me. My mother thinks I should go to college. "You won't be able to live off the movie deal forever," she says as we get out of the car. "You need to have plans."

"I do have plans," I say. "I'm going to open a pet store near the zoo."

Sara Ann is writing furiously.

"All the other kids your age are in college. They're learning. You're acting crazy."

"You're unsupportive. All the other mothers your age let their kids do whatever they want."

Sara Ann sighs.

"What?" I ask.

"Nothing," she says.

"Are we too typical for you?"

"No," she says. But I know that she thinks we are. In the movie, we live in a run-down house with a car on blocks in the driveway. Sara Ann let me read the beginning of the script before I got outraged at how much they had changed everything. In reality, we live in a nice, small house. We're not trashy, although we're not rich or anything. But nobody in Stirling is rich. That doesn't mean we're idiots.

"What do you want us to do? This is how we talk."

My mother looks down and says, "Nice socks."

"They're Jill's," she says.

"I know," my mother says. "I bought them for her."

"Don't stretch them out," I say and try to give her the meanest look I can.

———

In the house, on top of the piano, there is a picture of my parents and a very pregnant me on the couch with Barbara Walters. Everyone is smiling except me, because the baby is kicking. I asked for the photo to be taken again, but by then, Barbara was up and out the door. She wasn't very sociable with us before or after the interview. Frankly, I think she was disappointed: I was just another stupid, trashy kid who got knocked up by her teacher. Nothing surprises Barbara.

In the movie version of our interview, I cry. Well, Sara Ann Schwartz playing me cries. She wants to discuss this scene with me.

"How did it feel to be interviewed by Barbara Walters?"

"It was more boring than I thought it would be."

"But she made you cry."

"Actually, she didn't."

"In the movie, you cry."

All of a sudden, I wish they were not making a made-for-TV movie of my life.

My mother serves whiskey and peanuts and the three of us sit together and sip. My mother tries to ask Sara Ann questions about Hollywood and the theater world, but Sara Ann only wants to talk about me. I only want to look for the change I hid in the sofa cushions before I moved out. As we all sit there in silence because nobody is talking about what anyone else wants them to, my mother winks at me. I bet she took all my quarters out from between the cushions.

"Bitch," I say.

She looks at me as if she doesn't know what I'm talking about.

"Don't you know that's where I save all my change?" I say, gesturing to the sofa.

She shrugs her shoulders. "I thought it was mine," she says.

I get up to go to the bathroom. After I leave the room, they start talking. I go to the one in the kitchen so I can still hear what they are saying. That bathroom is decorated with my mother's artwork—she paints noodles in neon colors and glues them to pieces of cardboard. Every year, she has a booth at the Stirling Crafts Fair and nobody buys anything. "I'm just too cutting edge for these small-town minds," she says. I have two of her pieces up in my apartment and one in my ticket booth at the zoo. Someone asks at least once a day if it was made by the monkeys. I tell them matter-of-factly that it was made by my mother, Felicity Baker, and is for sale for the bargain price of seventy-five dollars. They always laugh and say something about monkeys throwing their shit. But fuck them. It's my mother's art, after all.

In any case, while I'm in the bathroom, I hear my dad come home.

"Felicity, I'm home," he says.

"Hello, Bill," my mother responds. I am examining my eye gunk in the mirror. "Jill's here."

I hear him walk into the living room. "Hi, Jill," he says. "How's the new place?"

"Great," Sara Ann says in her clipped imitation of me.

"And the zoo?"

"Peachy!"

"Good to hear, sweetie." Then, I hear him drop his briefcase. "You're not Jill!"

"Oh no…I'm just playing her in the movie…," she says, reverting to her Sara Ann accent.

I wonder if she is embarrassed. I wonder if he is shocked. He does pause for a second. I crinkle up my eyes to see where my wrinkles are going to be.

"Bill Baker. You're good. Just elongate your vowels a little. And Jill would never say 'peachy'. She'd say, 'Fucking awesome'."

"You're right," Sara Ann says. "Thanks."

"You could be her sister though. Wouldn't it have been nice to have another daughter, Felicity?"

I pop a tiny zit next to my nose and leave the bathroom without washing my hands.

"Duh," I say to myself on my way down the hall. "I think we need to go for a walk," I say to Sara Ann Schwartz when I get back to the living room.

"Good idea," she says.

We each put on one of my jackets and head out the front door.

After we walk in silence for a few minutes, she asks, "Well, what about the scene where Joe Rogers is convicted of statutory rape? How did you feel when the sentence was read?"

I paused and thought about that day. "I felt sad because my boyfriend was going to jail." Really, I was relieved that they had someone else to film and bug.

"So you really loved Joe Rogers?"

"No, but he was my boyfriend. He was going to jail. What was I going to do? I had just had a baby, it died almost immediately after it was born, my face was all over the news, nobody at school would talk to me. The only people who were interested in me were television producers and gossip columnists. Do you know what that feels like?"

"That must have been really hard." Sara Ann puts her hand on my shoulder.

"It was," I say. Now I am holding back tears.

"Do you ever wonder about the baby?"

"You mean, Dexter?" I say. Dexter would be two years old now. "But who cares! I'm nineteen years old. Who needs all that shit anyway?"

Sara Ann backs away from me. The school where it all went down is looming at the top of the hill. We are walking against traffic and all of a sudden, I realize that a car could speed around the bend and just hit us, send us flying off into the woods like inflatable dolls. And then how would the movie of my life get made? It's not going to be a great movie, but it'll be a movie, after all. I am going to be nicer to Sara Ann Schwartz.

"I'm sorry I snapped at you," I say, holding out my hand. She takes it. "It's hard for me sometimes, especially around his birthday. It's soon."

"I'm so sorry to hear that," she says. "We should do something to commemorate it. Maybe a session with a psychic. That's what I do when I'm feeling down. They usually tell you that things are going to be okay."

"That would be nice," I say.

—————

When we get back from our walk, Sara Ann and I each take showers and get ready for dinner, which my mother is making. She makes a mean meatloaf, you don't even need ketchup to get it to go down. As I am pulling on my jeans and Mickey Mouse T-shirt and Sara Ann is putting on hers, she comes over and stands behind me. She holds on to my shoulders and turns me to look in the mirror. She is wearing my favorite sweatshirt and her hair is stuffed into the hood. Without all that blonde hair, she actually does look a little bit like me.

"We'll be fucking famous together," she says in a decent imitation of me.

"I'm already famous," I say, trying to break free from her grip. But she won't let me go. I wiggle and squirm but she holds on tighter and tighter.

"But from now on, we'll be linked. People on the street might even think you're me and call you Sara Ann." She continues to hold my shoulder with one hand and strokes my hair with the other. I examine us in the mirror, me and someone trying to be me. She pulls me back toward her and kisses my neck, so lightly that I'm not even sure it is a kiss. Her lips are soft, but her grip on me is strong.

My heart stops. Up to now, a lot of thing have happened to me. At the time, I was all pissed off about being psychoanalyzed on *Court TV* and having my picture splashed across ABC for a week before my 20/20 interview, like, why were they invading my life? But now, I guess, part of me thinks it's kind of cool, now that it's all in the past. I mean, people totally recognize me at the mall. I even get fan mail. There's one guy who sends me birthday cards. All the people know me as Jill Baker. Even if they know me as Jill Baker, the girl who fucked her teacher. At least they know that it was an accident. I realize that Sara Ann Schwartz is still hugging me.

"No," I say, shaking her off. "People will call you Jill."

She shakes her head. "I'm not so sure."

"I am," I say.

"Well, there we disagree." She drops her hands to her side and unzips the sweatshirt to reveal the shirt I wore to the 20/20 interview, this button-down thing with a high collar that I thought would make me look grown-up. On Sara Ann, it just looks stupid.

"I guess we should go down to dinner," I say, shaking my head in disbelief.

"I guess."

"Screw you," I say as we walk down the stairs. I step more heavily than usual so she thinks that's how I really walk down the stairs.

———

Sara Ann and I sleep in my childhood bedroom, where I did everything from playing with dolls to losing my virginity to Vinny Capuano. She's on the top bunk, which I always figured was purchased for a sibling, but since I never had one, it was only used for occasional toy storage.

Sara Ann sleeps later than the rest of us. I surmise that it is because she has been up much of the night, rooting through my things. I thought I heard someone in the closet at around 3 AM, but it was too dark to investigate fully. I would have turned on the light to make sure, but I didn't want to wake Sara Ann Schwartz if she was still sleeping. I figured it was okay if she read my old elementary school diaries, they were just about how much I liked butterflies and ponies and Katie O'Callahan.

Before she comes down to breakfast, things are almost like they were before the whole Joe Rogers fiasco. My mother is yelling at my father about how bad he makes the bathroom smell when he shits. I am pouting and cutting my food into micro-sized bits so that I don't have to chew. This makes my mother more insane than the smelly bathroom. "Stop pulverizing your food!" she yells. I smile. Everything is right in the Baker house.

When Sara Ann comes down, we stop fighting. I am cutting up French toast with raspberry jelly and drinking black coffee. I normally prefer rye toast with marmalade, but my mother is out of marmalade and does not have rye bread. We are all eating quietly when Sara Ann enters the room. She has cut off her hair to be the same length as mine and has dyed it red. She is wearing the outfit that I wore the day before. It is a little bit big on her, but other than that, she looks exactly like me. My mother gasps. My father twitches. I scream.

"This is fucked up," I say when I am done screaming. The cats look up at Sara Ann. They wonder where this second Jill has come from. They nuzzle against her legs. She pets them. They purr. They like this Jill better than the real Jill. And I thought I was good with animals.

"Well, well," my mother says. "What would you like for breakfast, Jill?"

"Rye toast with, um, marmalade, please," Sara Ann says.

"I'll see if we have any," my mother says. She has told me just a half hour earlier that she does not have either of these things, but she produces both for Sara Ann. "You're in luck. I just happen to have that! Did you sleep well?" she asks.

"Like a fucking baby," Sara Ann says. She elongates her vowels.

"Me, too," I say. My mother ignores me.

"Do you want coffee with that?"

"Black, please."

"That's a coincidence," I say. Nobody responds.

"I like to fuck girls," I say. "I'm a lesbian." I have never said these words in this house before. Nobody hears me. It is as if I am invisible. I stand up and take off my clothes. Sara Ann takes her place in my chair.

"It's so good to have you here," my mother says to Sara Ann. "We see you so rarely lately."

"I was thinking I might go to college," I hear her saying as I run out of the room, naked and screaming. I run out into the middle of the road to see if I am really there. I need to know for sure because all of a sudden, I can't feel myself anymore. I stand on the double yellow line, my arms up in the air, screaming. Car after car passes me by. I can feel their speed on my skin, but none of them hits me. Either I have disappeared, or I have shrunk to the width of these double yellow lines, leading infinitely in both directions.

The Hearts We Got from a Used-Heart Lot

Farah Marklevits

Winter's potholes did them in, or road salt,
or maybe a defective part, a hidden past
collision under cherry, chrome, and wax—
God, remember when they hummed on asphalt?

Stopped—so quickly—ground to useless
separate parts, we said, stunned: "My heart
won't turn over," and "I'm stalled, too heavy
to roll in neutral to the yard." Teach us,

someone, please, the way to diagnosis.
I lay my hand on the bars of his ribs
and guess wrong. He dons worker bibs
and plays mechanic. Somehow we both miss

the grace of grease and how it makes things work.
We pumice ourselves to a clean, white hurt.

The Un-Art of Meandering

Lindsay Faber Chiat

Instead, these hard-fought sprints
toward a ground I imagined
would harvest, would unsink the glass-
bottomed fireflies buried lovingly
in shoeboxes over those years.
These plans come to me sometimes
as sinister machinations; others like an owl
returning for her hair. I don't care
to measure progress in inches,
as if doors to the floor would
one day swing open, the word *truth*
etched in a banister. This type
of *wait until,* of *remain here,* whether we are ever
doing ourselves any good
or just remembering who occupies
the spaces around us—
O sun,
bone-split patterns of jagged light
against our flat, unacquired selves. Proof
that at one time, we in the dark spaces
came together, quiet as beetles,
in an attempt to carry on.

Oregano is to Oregon

I do not know this yet but in three days I will harvest
plums from the pool. I say this entire sentence out loud
today, so as to predict the prediction, get ahead
of myself. Topsy-turvy
ambition. Unsunk cups. Brown hair in clotted bales:
texture is clearly at issue here. How to ascend
the air? Up the scaffold of astringent lace? You move
closer, say, *this is how to live,* as in grace, or a slow arc.
The unyielding, the purpling, the too-quick flight of night's rag.
And they who are accustomed, like a continual hit
to the bone, unraveling of the throat. Paired birds;
their fierceness and a step.

The Last Hour of Throats

Andrea Baker

The town that cast the largest shadow

lived in its own dark grace

and elegance there concealed
the great who gathered about the war

though the rivers outside were blank and weary

and the storm doubled as regret

and everywhere the dead were in need
of boxing
even if

they were still alive

The Haiku Garden

Karen Carissimo

Shiro stepped into the house his wife Ishi called the "flying saucer." What was intended to be an architectural feat looked like half a football lodged into the side of a hill. Wood beams propped up the front end of the house, and because of Ishi's worry, Shiro habitually surveyed the wood and surrounding soil for evidence of termite damage. Ishi was convinced that an armada of Formosans had been mounting a silent and invisible destruction, and at night while asleep, Shiro, Ishi, and their young son Takeo would tumble into the gorge below when the wood beams gave way.

Shiro stood at the curved wall of windows in the living room and looked out past Ohana Point to the flat blue ocean scarred by whitecaps. Instead of deflecting the glare, the tinted windows captured the morning sun and contained it until a miasma of heat moved through the house in the afternoon.

He went into the kitchen. Takeo sat at the table doing his math homework and picked at a bowl of lychees beside his open book. The boy looked at Shiro and mumbled a hello, then lowered his eyes back to his book. Ishi gave Shiro a curt nod and continued to busy herself in the kitchen. Since they had come to Hawaii, Ishi showed her resentment in small, quiet ways. She refused to learn English, lavishing all her devotion to Takeo and to the nightly Japanese soap operas blaring the shrill, histrionic voices of women ranting about lost love. Shiro moved toward the sink and stood close to Ishi. She smelled of burnt broccoli and breathed heavily in the heat. "Don't touch those," she said, leading Shiro away from the drying rack filled with tea cups to the tall glasses in the cupboard suitable for drinking water. "Wash your hands," she instructed. She spoke tenderly, as though she were leading a toddler to the toilet for the first time.

During their first two years in the islands, Shiro remembered returning late in the evenings after work to the comfort of Ishi and Takeo in this strange house. He enjoyed hearing the familiar sounds of home, the rice cooker exhaling steam and the frenzied noises of Takeo's video games. He remembered with a remnant of desire Ishi's flushed plump cheeks and the thin strands of damp hair clinging to the sides of her face. He even looked forward to her tired smile, an expression he had come to know as a sign of affection throughout the twelve years of his marriage. It meant they could be anywhere in the world, confronted with dizzying change, and the simple love that passed between the three of them would always tread the same triangular path.

———

They came to Maui in 1985, lured away from Japan by a booming economy. Shiro managed the white monstrosity of a hotel along the beach the locals referred to as the "Taj Mahal." That the new addition to the string of hotels studding the shoreline from Kihei to the acres of irrigated golf courses in Wailea was considered more than a little ostentatious did not deter plane loads of Japanese and Mainland tourists from paying the highest hotel rates anywhere on the island. Shiro preferred the tourists to the cranky businessmen he had tended to in the staid Osaka hotel he left behind.

Shiro knew he was alone in his happiness. Ishi had followed him here out of duty, leaving her mentally unstable mother Jin in the city. After Ishi's father died, Jin left her small cabin in Hokkaido and moved into the Osaka apartment. The woman began her subtle torment at once. He could see in Jin a quiet hysteria that expressed itself in a nebulous array of physical symptoms, headaches that had Jin in bed for days thinking she had a brain tumor, or a queasy stomach that must be a prelude to an agonizing death from cancer. Soon the illnesses, or threat of them, began to infect the household. Ishi looked after her mother with a solicitude that only validated Jin's endless complaints.

Poor Takeo, Shiro thought, with his childhood memories darkened by the pall and stench of old age. The boy was frightened of her, that was clear. On several occasions, Shiro woke in the night to hear the muffled sounds of Takeo crying. For a boy who was always emotionally composed, even a little withdrawn, the sight of him quivering like an injured animal was unsettling. "What was the dream this time?" Takeo held his father's hand and said, "It was the same lady with gray teeth. She was in my room." Shiro suspected the witch Takeo had dreamed about was his own grandmother. One night Takeo told Shiro about his dreams of death. "It comes at night and takes pieces of us when we sleep," Takeo told his father. "Death does no such thing," Shiro said. "It will come when you are an old man. Swift and sudden."

The old woman taxed them all, and Shiro could feel his family weakening under the strain of Jin. Ishi escorted Jin to doctors who always pronounced the woman of sound body. Her mind was another matter, but that, too, eluded diagnosis. Shiro could hardly bear Jin's weeping proclamations that her death was imminent, and how the knowledge of this was a torture that surpassed even the uncaring attitude of her son-in-law. Shiro could plainly see the woman was simply depressed and wanted to die, but those who want to die somehow end up aging well into actual infirmity, or at least long enough to exhaust the sympathies of their families. On their monthly drives north to the spas in the country, Shiro thought morbidly he could offer the woman exactly what she wanted, a turn of the wheel off a cliff and a quick death so Jin might carry her misery into her next life.

Excising Ishi from her mother's grasp was a task Shiro had come to dread. Shiro became like a sculptor chipping away at a block of stone, searching for the contours of his wife. The tropics would do them well, Shiro reasoned, though he barely discussed the matter with Ishi. During those last nights in Osaka, he no longer saw his wife's plain but pleasing face drifting through his mind as he edged toward sleep, but it was Jin's sagging eyes and pale lips that jolted him awake. If they stayed any longer in that apartment, Shiro was sure that Ishi would turn imperceptibly, then suddenly into that weary gray-toothed woman.

Like the tourists basking in an escape from their daily lives, Shiro in Hawaii felt wholly delivered from a cramped and common city life. Engulfed by such intense natural beauty, it was impossible not to feel he had abandoned a formerly demeaned existence. In his first giddy days touring Maui, Shiro felt certain that if there was a God, it had taken no notice of him until now.

When Shiro's job transfer came through, he wasn't exultant until Jin refused to leave Japan. Ishi resisted the move. "Who will take care of my mother?" she asked Shiro. He thought it best not to point out that it was Jin who took care of them all in her own peculiar way with her efforts to make herself indispensable around the house, yet draining the family with her insatiable needs.

Shiro first flew to Maui on his own to look for a house. He opened his suitcase to find a message typed on ornate stationery. It read: THE ONLY WESTERN PARADISE YOU WILL EVER FIND IS IN HEAVEN WITH AMIDA BUDDHA. There was no signature. It could only be from Jin, a woman who battled her depressive episodes with religious fanatacism. Shiro tore up the note and threw it away.

When Ishi first walked into the house in Haiku, she crossed the wood floors in the living room to the windows and sighed. Shiro noted the defeat in her limp shoulders and her downturned eyes. "It's crooked," she said, surprised. "The floor is crooked." Shiro walked toward her. If the floor sloped at all, he didn't notice the imperfection. Over the next few days she claimed to feel seasick. Her dizzy spells persisted when she came too close to the windows, so Shiro stood alone in the evenings mesmerized by the view.

Ishi cooked and cleaned all day while Shiro was at work. If she took any notice of the changes in scenery, in the landscape of her new life, she kept her observations to herself. In his rare moments of doubt, Shiro imagined she had carefully orchestrated her persistent despondence to cost him his happiness.

———

Shiro thought of those early days on the island in the garden off to the side of the house. It was a small piece of land he had fashioned into a perfect and contained world in miniature. Shiro had taken his inspiration for the garden from the carefully designed grounds at the resort. He dug a hole in the center of the yard for a pond with carp, and beside it, planted a lavish golden shower tree. He let the bougainvillea extend its thorny tendrils along the fences, so the yard was encased by a trimmed thicket of purple blossoms. Takeo understood its beauty, for he sat with his father often as they watched the fish writhe slowly in the clear water. The trees and shrubs were always ablaze with vivid flowers and brightly colored birds flitting among the branches. The arpeggios of birdsong and the feel of the brisk wind off the peaks of Haleakala into Haiku Valley guided Shiro into an effortless peace, a grace that removed him from Ishi's silent blame.

Since Ishi's English was bad and she rarely left the house except to shop, Takeo was her only source of companionship. She wrote and received weekly letters from Jin, and had no interest in urging Takeo off of the couch and into activities or friendships with other children. Takeo remained for two years by her needful side.

"Shouldn't he at least be watching American television?" Shiro said.

Shiro knew better than to try to push his son into sports or music. Takeo was not athletic, nor was he musical, at least to Shiro's impatient ear. In Osaka, Shiro endured eleven months of Takeo's practice sessions with the violin. Takeo returned home sullen each week after listening to the rebukes of his violin teacher, but his frustration stoked a rebellion that made his fervent playing sound like cats fighting in his room. Ishi thought she could hear scraps of melody interspersed through the caterwaul, but Shiro thought Takeo was too stiff to move in the way the instrument required to sustain any music. Ishi was angry when Shiro stopped the lessons.

"If he's upset, that's good," she said. "He's interested, and we must keep him so. That way he'll learn discipline."

"Which will happen first, the discipline or our souls being broken by that awful noise?"

"You're a selfish man."

Now Ishi kept Takeo comatose on the sofa to prove her point. It was odd that she would allow her son to become so average and unmotivated. So when Shiro got a phone call from Takeo's English teacher telling him his son won a poetry contest at school, he was elated.

———

Shiro and Ishi sat in Takeo's classroom waiting for his English teacher. When Annette Campbell entered the room, Shiro stood immediately. She was a petite woman with startling green eyes and pale skin. Annette smiled at him and Shiro sat down, embarrassed.

"So nice of you to come, Mr. and Mrs. Takashiyama."

Shiro was amused by the sound of his name americanized by her accent. "I was worried when you asked us to meet you."

"No need for that." Annette tossed a strand of wheat colored hair behind her shoulder. "Takeo's doing well in his classes. He's a little slow in his English skills, but he's very interested in science."

"He watches too much television. The Japanese station." Shiro laughed nervously.

Annette looked at Ishi, but Ishi looked away, her hands clasped in her lap.

"Well, Takeo is so bright he'll be able to catch up easily with a tutor," Annette said.

Shiro leaned forward in his chair, unable to hide his delight that this lovely woman would take a special interest in his son. "What about this poetry contest?"

Annette's face lit up with pride. "We've been studying Kipling and several haiku poets, such as Basho and Moritake. Not surprisingly, the kids prefer the short poems. But Takeo has shown unusual depth and maturity for a fifth grader." Annette handed Shiro the poem. Shiro read aloud:

The pheasant looks lost
hobbling up the mountain--
An old man near death.

"Very clever," Shiro laughed.

"I thought so," Annette said.

Shiro recited the poem in Japanese to Ishi and she smiled, nodding to Annette.

"Would you consider tutoring my son?" Shiro asked.

Annette hedged a little. "I'm not sure that would be fair to the other students."

"I know Takeo would benefit from your influence," Shiro said decisively. "Your meetings with him could be entirely confidential." His smile conveyed the warmth of his attraction to her, and she relented.

"I'd be happy to help your son," she said. She stood and shook hands with Shiro, nodding to Ishi.

On the way home, Shiro stopped at a stationery store and bought a leather-bound composition book. They found Takeo on the sofa watching TV. Shiro strode across the room and switched it off. He gave Takeo the journal and a shiny silver pen. "For my son, the poet."

———

Shiro and Takeo began to spend many days in the garden together, and Ishi joined them occasionally, taking delight in Takeo's new hobby. Takeo loved to feed the carp and watch their tiny mouths grab for the specks of food. He liked to sit on the smooth rise of stone beside the pond and look into his notebook, pushing his round glasses to keep them from falling off his small nose. Shiro watched Takeo frown at the blank pages.

"You have to pay attention to what's around you," Shiro said, "then catch your thoughts before they fly off."

"Like butterflies," Takeo said.

"Exactly." Shiro smiled and clipped the bougainvillea hedge. He had ordered a row of gardenias, and admired the contrast of the glossy green leaves against the ghostly white petals. Against the house they waited in their orange plastic pots to be planted.

———

Shiro often picked up Takeo at school late in the afternoons. He would find Annette and Takeo reading together.

"I wish all my students could be like Takeo," Annette said one day.

Shiro felt proud. "How is he different from the other kids?"

"Takeo is special," she said. "He's mature, but also more innocent than the other children. And he accepts his own uniqueness, even if it isolates him."

"Does he seem happy?"

Annette paused. "Yes," she said, "but not in a thoughtless or carefree way. He seems to be aware that happiness is a mood, and not a permanent state of being."

"Is there anything I can do to help him?"

"Well, I think he's adjusting fine. I guess we should just let him be."

Shiro took note of her use of 'we', and his curiosity was aroused. "I'm afraid Takeo might be taking too much time away from your own family."

"Oh, I'm divorced. I also have a son. He lives with his father in California, but he likes to visit me here in the islands."

Over the next few weeks, Shiro continued to meet with Annette to talk about Takeo's progress. Shiro liked how she mirrored his enthusiasm and cared for his son.

———

After Ishi and Takeo went to sleep, Shiro stayed awake and sat beside the pond. He read the poetry books Annette had given him. Lines of Basho ran through his mind: *Very brief: / gleam of blossoms in the treetops / on a moonlit night.* Shiro loved Basho's wit and charm, his sentiment grounded by loneliness. He went into the house and watched Takeo sleep, thinking of the lines: *Sad nodes— / we're all the bamboo's children / in the end.* Ishi would think Shiro had gone mad if he woke her in the middle of the night to recite lines of poetry, so he collected them throughout the week, typed them, and folded them into Annette's mailbox.

———

"Your house is so perfectly you," Annette said.

Shiro laughed. "My wife would agree."

Annette pressed her hand to the warm glass in the living room. As she moved to the side door that led to the garden, Shiro wiped away her hand-print with his shirt.

"Where's Ishi?"

"She took Takeo to the market."

"So they'll be back soon."

"Yes."

Annette went outside. Shiro followed her. She stood by the golden shower tree. The sun lit her hair with a coppery hue. "It's spectacular."

"Just the tree?"

"All of it," Annette said. Her face suffused with pleasure, as if Shiro had just given her a special gift. "I've never wanted to belong anywhere. But I could belong here."

She knelt at the pond and tapped her fingers over the surface of water. The fish darted wildly. "Why Basho?" Annette said. "Why is he your favorite?"

"He was a wandering soul. A man who saw every experience in life as a journey to some greater inner awareness. His explorations as a traveler strengthened him as a poet and as a man."

"Have you revealed something important about yourself to me?"

Shiro shrugged. "I think so."

"The poor guy," Annette said, "his little house burned down twice, I think. It's amazing he could remain so detatched from it all."

"Yes, but Basho had his banana tree. That made him happy."

"The poems you leave for me at school are beautiful."

"I wish I had written them. They express my need for you."

"Here's a poem that expresses my feeling. It's by Issa: *I'm going out / flies, so relax / make love.*"

Shiro lay beside Annette. All afternoon in the humid air, in the oddly dry sheets of her bed, Shiro pictured himself as a small animal burrowing into a pillow of straw. As he shifted his head toward her warm face, her long thick hair rustled against his ear like buckwheat hulls.

Annette got up and boiled a pot of coffee on the stove. Shiro didn't mind the feel of grounds on his lip as he drank. He admired how Annette's life had been pared down by necessity. Shiro had never seen someone so happy with so little. She kept her bed with the white quilt neat and her bathroom clean. The kitchenette looked onto a small dirt patio hemmed in by hibiscus hedges. Occasionally a pheasant walked past her window and Shiro would think of Takeo's poem. After a divorce and fitful searches for employment, she had ended up here, in a small in-law at the base of a volcano, teaching his son how to read and write poetry. In the dark they sat at her wobbly kitchen table under a bulb covered by a globe of rice paper. They talked softly, as though Ishi's ear might be pressed against the door.

"I lived in a rental car for two weeks when I first got to the islands," Annette said. "It was 1977. My doctor husband probably didn't notice that I'd left until the divorce papers arrived at his doorstep."

Shiro thought of the son she had left behind. "I'm sure he noticed," he said quietly. Like him, her destination was less important than the search itself for whatever was missing in her life.

———

They walked in a secluded forest of redwoods high upcountry and made silly faces at the bug-eyed cows who watched motionless as they passed. At the vineyard near Annette's cottage, Shiro bought her bottles of wine which she understood were never to be opened unless he was with her.

Annette never asked about Ishi, but Shiro sensed that Annette knew how much his wife anchored and sheltered him. He was cared for in a way that Annette had not known in ten years of wayward living. Being with Shiro made Annette feel likewise protected by Ishi's simple, unquestioning ways.

Shiro brought his lover food cooked by his wife. They ate Ishi's fish soups and meat stews.

"She cooks only for the winter," Shiro told Annette as they sweated over bowls of dumpling soup. "She makes no cold salads or sandwiches. She thinks she's still living in her snowy girlhood in Hokkaido."

"She probably is," Annette said.

"Ishi lives elsewhere in her mind, no matter what's around her. I could have taken her to the moon and she wouldn't have noticed. She's immune to everything, even me."

Shiro finished his meal and went outside. The night air had cooled. In the small yard beside the cottage, the grass was pocked and uneven. The stars were barely visible through the fog that tumbled down the hillside and frothed in the gorge below.

Through the rangy hibiscus hedge he could see his own house at the foot of the volcano. His wife and son were surely asleep by now. He felt distanced from them, from all the people, cities, and jobs that had once defined him. The thought of Japan had begun to recede into a distant reserve of memory, its sights and smells diminished by time and only briefly summoned by events in his present life. He thought of Osaka, the city he had once thought of as home. Living now in paradise meant that he was removed from the pointless human interaction that city life required. His footing on the grass felt uneven, the slope of ground making him feel as though he might pitch forward to his darkened house at the foot of the volcano.

He heard Annette's soft indistinct steps approach. Her arms around his waist and her breath at his ear made his mind swim with confusion. The air carried a heavy perfume of night-blooming flowers. The odor made him faintly sick. He feared that if he turned around he might not recognize the woman beside him, as he did not recognize his own skin made pale by the moonlight.

———

Takeo sat in the garden as the breeze turned chilly before dusk. Shiro weeded the edges of lawn. A wind drew breath and blew across the valley. Takeo sat at his usual spot on the stone. He wrote:

The wind's hands reach out
over many ocean miles—
my home has found me.

He read it aloud.

"Very nice," Shiro said distractedly.

"I miss Grandma," Takeo said.

Shiro ignored the comment and continued wrestling with the tough thready weeds. He'd neglected the bougainvillea. The bushes had grown far past the fence line.

"Do you think we'll all die like the dinosaurs?" Takeo said as Shiro stopped his tugging.

"No one's going to die."

"I saw it on TV. The earth is going to burn up in five hundred million years."

"That's a long time from now, Takeo."

Shiro felt he was fighting a losing battle. The gardenias had died in their plastic pots. He could scarcely believe that he was the man who had lain the sod, lodged bulbs deep in the moist earth, kept the pond so clean the water reflected all it could see.

———

"I'm lonely," Ishi told Shiro as she arranged the sheets on their futon. Shiro stopped her deft hands and held them. Ishi looked girlish and lost. She embraced Shiro.

"You haven't wanted me for so long," Shiro said.

"I should never have left Japan."

"Hasn't enough time passed?" Shiro untied the knot on her robe. "Can't I be your comfort?"

Ishi let the question linger. Their lovemaking was as awkward and rushed as on their wedding night, but an air of indifference replaced the once joyous curiosity that fueled their love many years ago. Ishi lifted the sheet to cover their bodies. They lay awake in the dark.

"So you love Takeo's teacher," she said.

Before Shiro could wonder what stray word or deed Ishi had used to unravel his mask of lies, she said, "She won't make you happy. Nothing will. Not a place, or a person."

"You seem to know me better than I know myself." Shiro was unable to keep the anger out of his voice. "I guess it was you who buried that silly note in my suitcase."

"Of course," Ishi said.

"How did you know?"

"You forgot all about the garden."

The next day Ishi picked up Takeo from school and checked into a hotel, leaving Shiro alone in the house.

———

The branches of the golden shower tree that draped over the little pond were bare. The yellow petals Takeo had said looked like a thousand butterflies covering the tree now floated on dingy water. Takeo sat at the edge of the pond. Shiro followed his son's gaze to the carp waving beneath the uneven blanket of petals.

"You spent so much time here writing your poems," Shiro said. "You're going to miss the beautiful yellow tree I planted for you, aren't you?"

"Not really."

Shiro nodded. "You'll be back for the holidays, though, and I'll visit you in Osaka. Annette wants to know you better. What do you think of her?"

"She looks young."

Shiro waited for his son to elaborate, but Takeo's usual grave expression revealed nothing. He looked at his father. "Did you know the earth is getting hotter and the Arctic is melting?"

Shiro laughed and shook his head.

"It's true," Takeo said.

"You shouldn't watch so much television, Takeo. It gives you bad dreams."

Ishi walked across the garden. "Say goodbye to your father." Shiro bent down and Takeo hung his arms loosely around his father's neck. The boy let go and ran to the house. Ishi gestured to the tree and shook her head. "You should have planted something that would keep its color."

Her face looked calm in the muted winter light. Shiro was troubled by malformed thoughts as he regarded his wife. Beneath her serene exterior, Shiro could see she was happy about returning to Japan. Her obvious relief felt to Shiro like a punishment for the crude, insignificant desires that had led him away from his family.

"Are you glad to be rid of me?" he asked.

She looked impatiently at him and smiled, not to demonstrate her sudden power over him, but simply because she had no words to satisfy him. Shiro wanted to know how many nights of tears it had taken for Ishi to accept that their marriage had failed. If he asked her this, she might say that she had cried many nights in an effort to forget him, but he would know she was lying.

———

Annette entered the house and approached Shiro in the glass-walled living room. Shiro thought it was right that he, a man who would send his family away, should remain in the house that Ishi had said was not properly rooted to the ground.

"Will you miss him?" Annette asked.

What could Shiro say? Maybe a clumsy friend would ask such a question, but not the lover who knew his thoughts and moods, who could answer every one of his unspoken regrets with suggestive silences of her own. The mention of Takeo on the day of his departure from Shiro's life could elicit only a bitter reply. He said nothing. They watched the sun spread a reddish haze over the rolling green landscape. Dusk spread quickly as they sat beside each other suspended above the valley below, the coming fog absorbing the view of hills and pasture and the ocean beyond.

Contributors.

Kirsten Andersen earned her MFA in creative writing from New York University. She has been awarded fellowships from the Fine Arts Work Center in Provincetown, MA, the Edward Albee Foundation in Montauk, NY, and the Rhode Island Council for the Arts. Her work has appeared in *Swink, Barrow Street, Greensboro Review,* and other journals. Currently a Wallace Stegner fellow at Stanford University, she lives in San Francisco, CA. ❧ **Andrea Baker** was the recipient of the 2004 Slope Editions Book Prize for her first book, *like wind loves a window.* She is also the author of the chapbooks *gilda* (Poetry Society of America, 2004) and *gather* (moneyshot editions, 2006). She maintains a Lyricism Blog at andreabaker.blogspot.com. ❧ **Jasper Bernes** was born in Southern California in 1974. Recent poems can be found in *The Canary, Bayou, La Petite Zine, Xantippe,* and in *The Iowa Anthology of New American Poetries.* He lives in the Bay Area with his girlfriend Anna Shapiro and their son, Noah, and is currently working on his PhD in twentieth-century poetry at UC Berkeley. ❧ **e. bojnowski** is a writer/musician/craftinoid from Magic Land and spends the days writing poems, drinking tea, daydreaming, crafting, and playing with the band Polyphonic Monk. ❧ **Boogie** was born and raised in Belgrade/Serbia. He lives in Brooklyn, New York. www.artcoup.com ❧ **Claudia Burbank** is the recipient of a Fellowship from the New Jersey State Council on the Arts, as well as a Pushcart Prize nomination. Her recent poems are published or forthcoming in *Prairie Schooner, Southern Poetry Review, 42opus,* and *New York Quarterly.* ❧ **Karen Carissimo** has poems appearing in *North American Review, Western Humanities Review, Atlanta Review, Cimarron Review, Calyx,* and elsewhere. Her fiction has appeared in *Green Mountains Review.* ❧ **Lindsay Faber Chiat** is a former New York City crime reporter whose news writing has appeared in several newspapers and magazines throughout the country. A graduate of Columbia University and the University of Pennsylvania, she lives with her husband in Brooklyn, NY. Recent poems appeared in *Barrow Street* and *The Salt River Review.* ❧ **Adam O. Davis** has poems appearing or forthcoming in *The Paris Review, Guernica, Western Humanities Review,* and an anthology of ekphrastic verse, *The Eye of the Beholder: A Poet's Gallery.* He lives in Brooklyn. ❧ **Bronwen Densmore** lives in Philadelphia. By day she works at a women's art college and by night she attends library school. She is looking forward to a long career of wearing sensible shoes and asking people to lower their voices. Between the hours of five and six AM, and when work is slow she writes poems, some of which can be found in journals such as *Fence*, *The Harvard Review*, *The Literay Review*, and *Pool*. ✤ **Linh Dinh** is the author of two collections of stories, *Fake House* and *Blood and Soap*, and three books of poems, *All Around What Empties Out*, *American Tatts*, and *Borderless Bodies*. His work has been anthologized in *Best American Poetry 2000 & 2004*, and *Great American Prose Poems from Poe to the Present*. He is also editor of *Night, Again: Contemporary Fiction from Vietnam*, *Three Vietnamese Poets*, and translator of *Night, Fish and Charlie Parker, the poetry of Phan Nhien Hao*. ✤ **Jeffrey Douglas** grew up and lives in Long Beach, California. His fiction has been published in *Vulcan: A literary Dis-alusion*. ✤ **Deborah Eshenour** wrote her first story at age eight, a mystery inspired by the *Trixie Belden* books. A recent graduate from Queens University of Charlotte's Creative Writing MFA program, Deb is seeking representation for her novel, *The Thousandth Man*, and is working on a creative nonfiction novel about the mysterious death of her uncle. She is an editor and writing teacher in Charlottesville, VA. This is her first publication. ✤ **Jacob I. Evans** is a writer and an artist. His work has been published in *Nocturnes (re)view, Goetry, Parthenon West Review, The Walrus,* and *Watchword*. He sits on the editorial board of Small Desk Press. He is an avid fan of sad music. ✤ **K. Goodkin** loves reading, writing, and talking about reading and writing. She lives in Chicago. ✤ **Noah Eli Gordon & Joshua Marie Wilkinson** live in Denver, CO. Wilkinson is the author of two book-length poems: *Suspension of a Secret in Abandoned Rooms* and *Lug Your Careless Body out of the Careful Dusk,* which won the 2005 Iowa Poetry Prize. Gordon is the author of five books, three of which are forthcoming, including: *Novel Pictorial Noise* (selected by John Ashbery for the 2006 National Poetry Series) and *A Fiddle Pulled From the Throat of a Sparrow*. Other selections from their collaborative book are forthcoming from *New American Writing, Lungfull, Cab/ Net, Small Town,* and *Word for Word*. ✤ **Mercedes Lawry** was born and raised in Pittsburgh, PA and has lived in Seattle almost thirty years. She's published poetry in such journals as *Poetry*, *Rhino*, *Nimrod*, *Poetry East*, *Seattle Review*, and others. She's received awards from the Seattle Arts Commission, Hugo House, and Artist Trust, and she's been a Jack Straw Writer and held a residency at Hedgebrook. Currently, she is the Communications

& Marketing Manager at the Museum of History and Industry. **Joanne Lowery's** poems have appeared in many literary magazines, including *Birmingham Poetry Review*, *5 AM*, *Passages North*, *Atlanta Review, One Trick Pony*, and *Poetry East*. Her chapbook *Diorama* was the winner of the Poems & Plays 2006 Tennessee Chapbook Prize. She lives in Michigan. **Farah Marklevits** lives in Cortland, NY, and teaches at Syracuse University. Her poems appear in *Three New Poets*, a collection published by Sheep Meadow Press, as well as in journals such as *Cimarron Review, Born Magazine, Poet Lore*, and *Octopus*. **Keya Mitra** received her MFA in fiction at the University of Houston, where she is currently a PhD candidate. Her work has appeared in *Ontario Review, Orchid, Gulf Coast, Best New American Voices 2007*, and *Confrontation*, and is forthcoming in *Event*. Her short-story collection was a finalist for the Mary McCarthy Prize this year. She worked as a fiction editor for *Gulf Coast* for two years and recently received a Fulbright grant to study creative writing in India. **Matthew Modica** has published stories in the *Beloit Fiction Journal* and *Mississippi Review* (online) and has received a fellowship to the MacDowell Colony. He lives in Portland, Maine. **Raymond Nolan** is a graduate of the Iowa Writer's Workshop. He has a story forthcoming in *Cadillac Cicatrix*, and lives with his wife and two kids in Florida. **Miriam Parker**, originally from New York, is pursuing her MFA in Creative Writing at the University of North Carolina at Wilmington. Her nonfiction work has been published in *The New York Press*, *The Brooklyn Rail,* and the anthology *2Do Before I Die*. This is her first published story. **Theo Rigby** received a degree in Documentary Photography from the Academy of Art University in San Francisco. He produces long-term social and political documentary projects and teaches photography. Clients include *Newsweek*, *The New York Times*, *National Geographic France*, *People*, *French Elle*, *The Sunday London Times*, and others. His photographs have been exhibited at San Francisco City Hall and at the 2005 Visa Pour L'Image festival in Perpignan, France. **Sandra Simonds** is a PhD student at Florida State University. Her poems have been published in many magazines including *Pool, the Colorado Review, the Seneca Review,* and *Barrow Street*. She is the editor of *Wildlife,* an experimental poetry magazine. **Pete Spence**, Born Melbourne, Australia in 1946. Living a totally interesting life to date. **Robert Strong** is the author of *Puritan Spectacle* (Elixir Press) and the editor of *Joyful Noise: An Anthology of American Spiritual Poetry* (Autumn House, March 2007). He lives north of the

Adirondack Park in New York State. ☙ **J.R. Toriseva** has taught at Mills College and Build. Currently, she works for Literary Arts. Her most recent work appears in PrismInternational. ☙ **Tony Tost** is the author of *Invisible Bride* (LSU 2004), winner of the Walt Whitman Award, and *World Jelly* (Effing 2005). His next book, *Complex Sleep & Other Writings* is forthcoming from University of Iowa Press in the fall of 2007. He lives in Durham, North Carolina where he edits *Fascicle* and is working on a PhD in English at Duke. ☙ **Andrew Touhy** was born in Chicago and grew up in Ft. Lauderdale, FL. His fiction has appeared or is forthcoming in *New Orleans Review*, *Quarter After Eight*, *Gulf Stream*, and other literary periodicals. Artwork based on "Another True Love Story" appeared in *The Whole Story*, a life-sized multimedia installation sponsored by Watchword Press. He lives and works in San Francisco. E-mail him at nank73@hotmail.com.

cimarron review

Subscription Rates

$24 per year ($28 outside USA)
$48 for two years ($55 outside USA)
$65 for three years ($72 outside USA)
Single Issues: $7.00 ($10.00 outside USA)

Submission Guidelines

Accepts submissions year round in Poetry, Fiction, and Non-Fiction

Simultaneous Submissions Welcome

205 Morrill Hall • Oklahoma State University • Stillwater, OK 74078
cimarronreview@yahoo.com • http://cimarronreview.okstate.edu

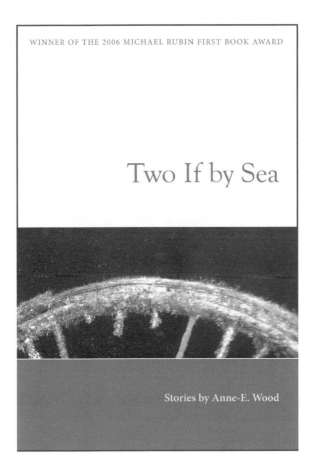

WINNER OF THE 2006 MICHAEL RUBIN FIRST BOOK AWARD

Two If by Sea

Stories by Anne-E. Wood

Two if by Sea by Anne-E. Wood

"These stories go off like fireworks. Anne-E. Wood's writing is fierce, tender, reckless, precise, alarming, lovely, and unforgettable." -Michelle Carter

Fourteen Hills Press

www.spdbooks.org

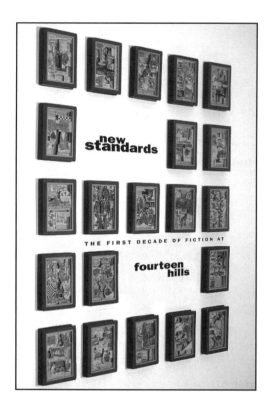

A new anthology commemorating *Fourteen Hills'* ongoing dedication to innovative fiction.

Stephen Elliott
Peter Orner
Eireene Nealand
Pam Houston
Robert Glück
Nona Caspers
John Cleary
Pamela Ryder
and many more

Available now on Amazon or from Small Press Distribution

www.spdbooks.org

Subscribe

✚ Please circle one. Prices include shipping and handling.

Single Issue (current): $9

One Year (two issues): $17

Two Years (four issues): $32

Institutional (one year): $24

Back Issues (please specify) Vol 1.1-9.1: $5
                                         Vol 9.2-12.2: $7

Volume_____ No. _____Qty_____

Name _____

Street Address _____

City _____ State/Province _____

Zip/Postal Code _____ Country _____

Phone _____ E-mail _____

Please enclose a check payable to Fourteen Hills: The SFSU Review and mail to:

Fourteen Hills
Department of Creative Writing
San Francisco State University
1600 Holloway Avenue
San Francisco, CA 94132-1722